THANKS
FOR
WAITING

THANKS FOR WAITING

THE JOY (& WEIRDNESS) OF BEING A LATE BLOOMER

DOREE SHAFRIR

BALLANTINE BOOKS
NEW YORK

Thanks for Waiting is a work of nonfiction. Some names and
identifying details have been changed.

Published in the United States by Ballantine Books,
an imprint of Random House, a division of
Penguin Random House LLC, New York.

BALLANTINE and the HOUSE colophon are registered trademarks
of Penguin Random House LLC.

Hardback ISBN 978-0-593-15674-2
Ebook ISBN 978-0-593-15675-9

PRINTED IN CANADA ON ACID-FREE PAPER

randomhousebooks.com

2 4 6 8 9 7 5 3 1

First Edition

Art by iStock/Nata_Slavetskaya

To Matt and Henry, who were both worth waiting for

INTRODUCTION

I recently came across an email inviting people to my thirtieth birthday party. I wasn't taken aback by the location (a karaoke studio in Manhattan's Koreatown) or the guest list (practically everyone I'd ever met), but I was shocked by the start time: ten P.M. I tweeted about it, writing, "Truly was I ever so young?"

The responses surprised me. My friend Caroline wrote, "My 30th birthday started at 5 P.M. and it was on a Monday and my invitation clearly stated, 'I am leaving the bar and going home at 7 P.M.'" Another woman said hers started at noon. Yet another—who has a baby almost exactly my son's age but is ten years younger than me—said, "I was literally never that young."

And then it hit me. Thirty *was* "old" to have a late birthday party! But how had everyone else gotten these parties out of their systems when they were twenty-four, if they'd ever had them at all? Meanwhile, on the night I turned thirty, I was blissfully shrieking into a microphone, drunk on cheap beer and too-strong vodka sodas in plastic cups. I wasn't engaged or married or pregnant. I lived in a small basement apartment. I had a job, but less than a year before, I had been an intern.

At the time, not having achieved any of the milestones I associated with "being an adult" didn't bother me, but as my early thirties turned into my midthirties and then my late thirties, I started to feel like I had been left behind, that everyone else's lives had moved on and progressed, and I was still the female Peter Pan singing a slightly off-key version of Mariah Carey's "We Belong Together" (deceptively tough karaoke song; still brings down the house every time). For men, there's just not as much pressure to do things on a timeline; the image of the man who takes an especially long time to "find" himself is one that has long been enshrined, even venerated, in our collective cultural consciousness.

But most women aren't afforded the luxury of doing things on their own time. The paradox of femininity is that we're always either too young and inexperienced, or too old and washed up. As my friend Maris Kreizman once put it on Twitter: "You're told you're young until you turn 35. By the time you're 40 you're over the hill. I had no idea at the time that I would only have 5 years to be the age when I was just a person."

Statistics do, in fact, point to the late thirties as being this turning point, where suddenly, more of your friends will be married, own homes, and have kids. So for those of us who *don't* hit that trifecta—what then? What if we want those things, but they just haven't happened for us, for whatever reason? Or if we don't want those things, but we feel like we *should*?

I've wrestled with all these questions. I got married at thirty-eight, had my first kid at forty-one, and undoubtedly will be renting in the very overpriced city of Los Angeles until the end of time. I also feel like I very much did *not* have my shit figured out at thirty, or forty. Even now, at forty-four, I'm still figuring "it" out, whatever "it" is.

Long after my thirtieth birthday party, I realized that I always had been, and probably always would be, "late"—to dating, to sex, to marriage, to motherhood, to finding the kind of work I truly like to do, to being comfortable in my own skin. And so I wanted to write this book as a gentle corrective to the idea that we're supposed to do things on a schedule. I'm only just becoming the person I was meant to be—and that took a lot of self-reflection and more than a little reckoning with the person I have always been. (And to be clear, that person is still a work in progress.)

But this book is not just about coming to terms with being a late bloomer; it's also about how I came to deeply *appreciate* it. Because sometimes coming-of-age happens on our own time—and that's okay.

PART ONE

CHAPTER ONE

It was the beginning of June 2009, and maybe the only surprising thing about the layoffs was that they hadn't happened sooner. The economy had tanked the previous fall, the United States was now officially in a recession, and *The New York Observer*, the newspaper where I'd worked for almost two years, was struggling. Its longtime editor, Peter Kaplan, had just quit, and the rumor was that he had chosen this moment to leave because he knew layoffs were imminent and he couldn't bring himself to execute them.

The morning of the layoffs, I went into work with a creeping sense of dread. Peter's replacement was his deputy, Tom, whom I didn't have an especially close relationship with, and I worried that as he had made up the list of who would stay and who would go, I was on it.

What would I do if I got laid off? I was thirty-two—not old, certainly, but old enough that I was no longer a cheap hire. And besides, we were officially in the worst recession since the Great Depression. "They're calling people into Peter's old office," I Gchatted my boyfriend, Jon. "I just don't have a good feeling about this."

"Whatever happens, we'll figure it out," he responded.

But I didn't want to "figure it out." I wanted to keep my job—not just because getting fired in the middle of a recession is not exactly ideal, but also because getting hired at the *Observer* had been a dream come true. When I was in college in Philadelphia, I had become obsessed with the paper, an oversized, salmon-colored weekly (Henry Rollins, perhaps apocryphally, had once called it "the curiously pink newspaper") where Candace Bushnell had written the "Sex and the City" column that had become the TV show. The paper, written in a droll, knowing, literary style, portrayed an alluring New York of socialites and magazine editors and hedge funders. I wasn't interested in actually being one of the people they wrote about—I wanted to chronicle and interpret this world, as a kind of Harriet the Spy of exclusive New York.

I got to write about pretty much anything I wanted: profiles of intense and weird politicians like Anthony Weiner, columns about what it was like when your deadbeat boyfriend got his life together after you broke up, trend stories about nerds who were actually jocks. Since I was a kid growing up outside of Boston I'd always been enamored with New York— for my fourteenth birthday, my mom and I drove to Manhattan and had lunch at the Rainbow Room in Rockefeller Center, which I thought was the height of sophistication; it felt like being literally on top of the world.

Now, thanks to my job, I had been given the keys to a New York world that felt exciting and exclusive, and, often, borderline absurd, like a party for a line of wine-related clothing accessories hosted by *60 Minutes* host Lesley Stahl (yes, this was an actual event that occurred). Most of my friends worked in media, too, and even though the scene could sometimes feel claustrophobic—you *did* tend to see the same faces at the book parties and the dinners and the launch events—it was also satisfying to feel like I had *made it.* But even outside of work, I just loved existing in the city. Everything was here, and I got to be a part of it.

I'D GOTTEN THE job a couple of summers earlier, when Peter, then the editor in chief, had emailed me to ask if I wanted to get coffee. At the time, I was working for the media gossip blog Gawker. Peter was a legend in New York media; it felt like I'd been summoned by the literary gods. He was known for hiring the best young reporters, writing the snappiest headlines, producing a must-read paper each week on a shoestring budget. I was dying to work for him.

"So how are things going over there?" he had asked when we sat down at Friend of a Farmer, a café down the street from the *Observer* office. He was wearing his trademark tortoiseshell glasses and a loosened tie, and khakis. His hair was graying, but he had a full head of it. The overall effect was rumpled professor.

"Well, Choire is a genius," I said, not really answering the question. Choire was Choire Sicha, the editor in chief of Gawker, who had left the *Observer* to take the Gawker job; he had previously left an earlier stint at Gawker to take the job at the *Observer.* He and Peter were still close. It was all very incestuous. Was Peter trying to get back at Choire for leaving by hiring me? And if he was, did it matter? I liked working for Choire, but I didn't feel any particular loyalty to Gawker, which was a notoriously difficult place to work, and after less than a year there I was already feeling burned-out. Still, I was mindful of performing the delicate dance of signaling my interest in a job, while not trashing my current employer, while also not wanting to appear desperate.

"Well, listen," Peter said, after we'd sipped our coffees and chatted for half an hour or so. "You've been doing terrific stuff with Choire. But—I think you should come to the *Observer.*"

I tried to keep my face looking pleased but not overly excited. "What kind of job are you thinking?"

"I'd put you on the 'Ideas' beat," he said. "Literary stuff, academia, the intellectual scene in New York. You'd have a lot of freedom. Think about it, okay?"

"I will," I said. "Before we go, I do have a question—I know most of the reporters are, like, twenty-four. I don't mean to put this indelicately, but can you afford me?"

Although I wasn't making a ton of money at Gawker, I was making more than twenty-two thousand dollars a year, which was what I had heard was the starting salary for *Observer* reporters. There was no way I'd be able to survive on that in New York—I didn't have a trust fund or family help, and I couldn't stomach the idea of going back to live in a crappy apartment with multiple roommates just to take this job.

Peter seemed embarrassed at the mere mention of money. "I think I can work it out, yes," he said.

I started a couple of months later. I was one of the older reporters in the bullpen, but it felt like I was finally where I was supposed to be.

AND THEN, in the fall of 2008, after I'd been at the paper for a little over a year, the economy crashed. The papers ran photo after photo of shell-shocked Lehman Brothers analysts leaving their offices with their company gym bags after they had learned the company would be shutting down. At first, it felt surreal: Surely the *whole* economy wasn't crashing? At the paper, we published a piece about "Crash Virgins," aka people who had never been through an economic crash before. But clearly, the economic crisis was running much deeper than just being a cute trend story. We just didn't yet know how deep, or how our lives would change.

The owner of the paper, Jared Kushner, the son of a disgraced New Jersey real estate magnate, long had been an infrequent but anxiety-producing visitor at work. But now he seemed to be showing up more often, wandering around the office and stressing everyone out, especially Peter. By January, the parties dried up, even more so than the usual post-holiday-party slump. Things at the paper were also getting more dire financially. Advertising was way down, and the shoestring budget that we'd been operating on got even more shoestring. I was now editing the paper's social column, "The Transom," but the paper's freelance and expenses budgets were slashed. I had to make the case for why my one remaining reporter should be reimbursed for the cabs she took home late at night from covering the few parties that were still happening. Still, even now, months into the crash, I wasn't overly concerned; the *Observer* had always operated on a shoestring budget, and I was confident that this, too, would pass.

But it didn't. And then Peter announced he was leaving, and there was a big farewell party at Elaine's, the Upper East Side bar and restaurant that had been a longtime gathering spot of a certain milieu of literary New York; it was festive but melancholy. The next day, people started getting called in to Tom's office.

After I Gchatted Jon, I messaged my former boss, Choire, who had since left Gawker and had started a new website called The Awl. "Tom wants to see me in his office at 12:30. What do you think that means? Do you know anything?"

"There was a list that I saw, but I don't think you were on it," he wrote back.

"Argh," I wrote. I wasn't sure if I believed him—if he *had* seen me on the list, would he tell me? But I just wanted it to be over, whatever it was.

Finally, it was noon, and I went into Peter's old office. Tom was there, along with another executive, Barry, whose job was nebulous but seemed to encompass HR functions. Tom was holding a folder; his hands were shaking. "We've decided to let you go," he said. I nodded and didn't say anything. He said a few other things, but I wasn't really listening; I was just thinking about how I wanted to get out of the office, which suddenly felt very hot, as quickly as possible. When I got back to my desk, there were cardboard boxes there to pack everything up.

Twelve people were laid off that day. After I packed my things, I stared at my desk, which until that morning had been messy with books and papers. It was now empty for the first time since I'd started. That morning, I'd woken up, gotten dressed, taken the subway in to work. A normal day. What would my days look like from now on?

"So long," I whispered, and walked out the door, trying not to cry. It felt like when someone breaks up with you and even if you've kind of been thinking that things hadn't been going *great,* you didn't think they had gotten all *that* bad, certainly not breakup bad, and then the person who an hour ago was your partner and is now your ex leaves and it's just *over,* and you think for a second that they're going to come back and tell you that it was all a mistake, they still love you, and then you have make-up sex and they bring you coffee in the morning. I didn't want to have make-up sex with the paper, but I half thought—hoped—that as I got on the elevator, someone would come running after me, breathless, to tell me it had all been a mistake, they meant to lay off *Tori Macfrir*, they just got confused, and could I just come back to my desk and work on a trend story about elaborate birthday parties?

AFTER YEARS OF grad school and jobs that never felt quite right, the *Observer* had felt, if not perfect, then something close to it. Now I was out of work, and at sea. I was slightly reassured by my boyfriend, Jon, telling me that we'd figure it out, but he worked in politics and didn't make much money either.

I felt like I was on the precipice of a Real Adult Life but it kept being just out of reach: I'd had a job, and now I didn't; Jon and I had been together for two and a half years, but we weren't engaged like I was hoping we would be by now; we lived in a brownstone apartment in a beautiful neighborhood in Brooklyn, but between the two of us and our dog, it was cramped, and it also had mice. (Our landlords, who lived upstairs, advised us to get a cat. I'm allergic.)

As I took the subway back to my apartment in Fort Greene, I wondered, was I asking for too much—to have a job *and* an engagement *and* a decent apartment in my thirties? Obviously there were many, many people who did not have any of these things, and to articulate that I wanted them felt entitled, like I deserved things that other people didn't. On the other hand, right now, I didn't have a job *or* an engagement *or* a decent apartment, and many people *did* have all of them. Why shouldn't I also be allowed to know what I wanted and try to get it?

I realized I had never been comfortable articulating exactly what I wanted—it made me feel too vulnerable, like I would be held accountable or people would pity me if it didn't work out. I couldn't allow my dreams to take up space in my own mind, so they couldn't take up space in the world, either. I knew that these anxieties were, on some level, irrational—even without really being able to talk about my big-picture ambition, I had still achieved a decent amount of success. Besides, most people are not keeping track of their friends' hopes and dreams, and if they are, they're usually not critical if they don't achieve them, unless their friends are assholes.

So maybe part of growing up was becoming secure enough in myself to articulate what I wanted. But if that was the case, I had a lot of growing up to do.

CHAPTER TWO

When it came to school, I wasn't a late bloomer. If anything, I was too much of an early bloomer, a precocious kid who was desperate to fit in and not be singled out for being smart. One day, when I was in kindergarten, I was playing with blocks with my friend Jodie. Suddenly, my teacher, Mrs. Gotkin, and a student teacher, Melissa, approached.

"Doree, it's time for you to go to the library to meet with Mrs. Zeigler," she said. "Melissa is going to walk you there."

I was confused—I was playing with blocks. I didn't want to be taken away from my friends, and I certainly didn't want to meet with a woman I didn't know in the school library.

"No," I said. "I don't want to go."

"You have to go," Mrs. Gotkin said.

"I don't want to go," I repeated. "I'm playing with Jodie."

Mrs. Gotkin and Melissa looked at each other. "Doree, you have to go."

I started crying. "I don't want to go!" I yelled, as Melissa picked me up and started carrying me out of the classroom. "Don't make me go!"

I cried as Melissa dragged me, literally kicking and screaming, to the library. It wasn't meant to be a punishment—I was getting extra time and attention because I could already read, and I was way beyond the kindergarten curriculum of learning letters and sounding out words. So Mrs. Gotkin had figured that my time would be better spent in the library, reading, which in theory was a neat solution for a student who had too much time on her hands. In practice, it made me feel awful: I didn't *want* to be singled out or made to feel special. Everyone else got to do these big, colorful workbooks that had an individual letter on the front of them, and as they finished the workbooks, they got hung up on the walls under their names. I didn't have any workbooks under my name, because I wasn't doing them. I didn't care that I could already read—I wanted to be doing the workbooks, like everyone else.

Mrs. Zeigler was an older woman with a kind face and dark brown hair. "So," she said, "I heard you like to read."

I nodded sullenly.

"I think I know some books that you might be interested in," she said, smiling. I begrudgingly took a look at the stack of books she had in front of her and then slowly started feeling a little better.

Soon, I wasn't mad about having to go see Mrs. Zeigler, even if I did still occasionally feel embarrassed about being singled out. She introduced me to Ramona Quimby and *Superfudge* and The Boxcar Children, and later to *Tuck Everlasting* and *Harriet the Spy*. I already loved to read, but I became obsessed with reading and kept books on my bed so I could easily access them again and again. Then I became obsessed with writing: I wrote, in longhand, books inspired by *Little House on the Prairie* and then, the summer I was seven, I got my first diary: It had Hello Kitty on the front, and more important, it had a *lock*. (Just to make sure that no one breached my defenses, I wrote PRIVATE! KEEP OUT! CONFEDENTIAL [*sic*]! TOP SECRET! THIS MEANS YOU! on the first page.)

Earlier that year, I'd read *Harriet the Spy*, which is about a precocious yet immature (and somewhat obnoxious) eleven-year-old New York City girl who carries a notebook everywhere she goes, scribbling observations about the people she spies on after school (a man with twenty-five cats, a divorcée confined to her bed, a family that owns a grocery), but also about her classmates. When they find her notebook, and read what she's written about them, they vow to take their revenge. It's a story about a girl who's a bit of a weirdo with a rich imagination, wise beyond her years in some ways but also very much still a child who eats only tomato sandwiches and is unhealthily attached to her nanny, who thinks she's smarter than almost everyone else and probably is, but that doesn't mean she knows anything about the world. Despite our differences (not limited to the fact that I hated tomatoes), I identified with Harriet completely, and so I needed a notebook of my own where I could write my own observations about my second-grade classmates: "Alyssa thought she could take over. I don't like her." "Person: Nina. Description: fat, smelly, black hair. Personality: nice, mean. Nina loves Christopher in our class." About my teacher, I wrote, "Personality: usually mean."

WE LIVED IN Brookline, Massachusetts, just outside of Boston, in a brown wooden house on a dead-end street. Brookline is now out of reach for people like my parents—single-family homes start at around $1.5 million—but in the early eighties,

you could be a junior college ESL professor (Mom) and tex-
tiles company middle manager (Dad) and afford it. They were
the kind of parents who were proud of the fact that the only
TV I watched as a kid, on a tiny black-and-white set, was *Ses-
ame Street,* and that I didn't know what a cookie was until a
babysitter gave me one. They got me a Holly Hobbie record
player when I was four and I listened to *Free to Be You and Me*
and the soundtrack to the *Annie* musical on repeat. Books
were everywhere, and before I was born, my mom had col-
lected into a three-ring binder all the Stories for Children that
ran in the back of *Ms.* magazine in the 1970s: stories like the
one about Deborah Sampson, who disguised herself as a man
so she could fight in the Revolutionary War, and a child named
X whose sex was a mystery.

My parents didn't seem like especially romantic people, but
the story of how they met sounded like it had been scripted in
a rom-com. Picture it: It's 1970. A pretty University of Michigan sorority girl takes a trip to Europe with her best friend the
summer before her senior year, but best friend bails halfway
through to go home to get married, right before the pair was
supposed to go to Israel. So the sorority girl finds herself staying alone on a kibbutz, a little bored, until the handsome red-
headed Israeli paratrooper who grew up on the kibbutz notices
her and invites her to tea. (I mean, *come on!*) They fell in love,
my mom finished up her senior year of college a semester early,
and went back to Israel to be with my dad, who was five years
older. They lived for a couple of years in a remote kibbutz on
the Lebanese border, but eventually made their way back to
the United States, got married, honeymooned in Greece, drove
a VW bug across Europe, and then, in 1977, they had me.

My dad never totally worked through his wanderlust, but

when you have three kids, I guess that just means you end up traveling a lot for work. I liked to look in his passport and see the stamps: the Philippines, Germany, the United Kingdom, Nigeria, Ecuador. Whenever he left, which was around once a month, he would be gone for a week or two and we would hear from him a couple of times, his voice sounding far away and staticky over the international long distance lines. He would always bring us back little gifts, sometimes things like a set of tiny figurines playing instruments he'd gotten in Nigeria, but more often than not, a bar of Toblerone chocolate. (For the longest time I thought that Toblerone was something you could only get in foreign countries.) We often didn't know exactly when he was going to be leaving for another trip until right before he left, which sometimes made planning things tricky. Was he going to be in town for my birthday, or my dance recital? Maybe, maybe not.

According to my parents, I had been shocked when they brought home my brother, Michael, a few months before I turned three. They also said I had never really gotten over not being an only child anymore. There's photographic evidence, too: In a Sears photo of us when I was around three and a half and Michael was still an infant, my face is set in a grimace, my eyes narrowed; Michael is smiling, clueless that his older sister resented his existence with every fiber of her three-foot-tall being. In another photo, taken at my grandparents' house, I'm sitting, grumpy, in the background while Michael crawls, blissfully unaware, in the foreground.

My sister, Karen, came along when I was days away from turning seven, and again I felt usurped: not just a younger sister, but they had given her a middle name, something that I didn't have and desperately wanted, because *everyone* had a middle name except me, *and* she was born six days before my birthday, thereby ensuring that hers would overshadow mine until the end of time. It seemed unfair. Why couldn't she have been born in literally *any* other month?

Once she got home, I ignored her. I had more important things to do, like finish first grade and go to swim lessons and tap dance class, than to hang around with a screaming, pooping baby. But she was, actually, hard to ignore. When she wasn't screaming or pooping, Karen was impossibly cute, one of those babies who gets stopped on the street and cooed at, with fair hair and blue eyes and a little button nose. Meanwhile, my so-called friend Nina was looking at my hair in our second-grade classroom and not liking what she saw. "Your hair's *stringy*," she informed me one day (maybe this was why I referred to her as "smelly" in my diary?). I touched my hair self-consciously. What did stringy hair feel like, anyway? My hair was just, well, hair: dark brown and straight, with a row of bangs across my forehead. But now, according to Nina, it was stringy, and therefore, not cute. I was suddenly hyperaware of my hair, and the fact of its not-cuteness.

THE IDEA THAT there was a specific way that girls were supposed to look and act, and things that they should be interested in, was really reinforced when I first went to sleepaway camp when I was nine years old. It was a Jewish camp on the shores of a small lake in southern New Hampshire, a little over an hour's drive from our house. My mom had gone there for one idyllic summer, twenty years before, and still talked about it wistfully. What I didn't totally grasp at the time was that my mom had been outgoing and popular—class treasurer, part of a self-named high school clique called the Wee Five—and I was more like my dad, reserved and slightly aloof, minus the thick Israeli accent.

We were Bunk Two, the second-youngest bunk of girls, and yet all the other nine-year-olds in my cabin seemed so much more mature. I barely felt like a tween, and they seemed like they were already deep into adolescence. They came with hair dryers and curling irons and lip gloss and wore Keds with slouchy socks like the older girls did, and by day three of camp had already loudly announced which of the boys they had crushes on, as though to claim them. The queen of the bunk was a girl named Rachel, from Long Island, who had long caramel-colored hair and a perpetual tan, and two older brothers who were also at camp. She and her friend Kim were the ones who plotted to ambush our counselor when she got out of the shower and pin her down on the bed, open her robe, and take a Polaroid, as though to say: *We rule this bunk, bitches.* Popularity meant power, or was it the other way around?

I loved some parts of camp—learning to water-ski, the campwide sing-alongs in the dining hall, rainy days when we'd stay in the bunk and write letters and play jacks—but the social aspects were challenging, even more so as we got older. The girls my age were neatly cleaved into the popular girls (as always, led by Rachel!), who had boyfriends and made sure to take all their electives together and saw one another during the school year and had inside jokes, and the rest of us. And yet I continued to go back to camp year after year, as though one summer I'd suddenly have a glow-up, and Rachel and her minions would finally induct me into their clique, and she'd share the secret pink memo, written in bubble letters with a heart instead of a dot over the *i,* that gave them specific instructions about to which summer to start bringing a razor to shave their legs, whether we were all wearing Umbros, how to talk to a boy to make him like you, and we'd make matching friendship bracelets in arts and crafts and mixtapes with "our" songs on our dual-cassette boom boxes and we'd all sit together on movie night, and of course, the Seths and Joshes and Bens in the boys' area would all want to go to the social with me.

Everything came into sharp relief the summer I was thirteen. For three weeks in July, I'd gone to a different camp—nerd camp, where I lived in a college dorm and took an essay-writing class and slow-danced to "Stairway to Heaven" with a boy from my class whom I had a huge crush on. I *loved* it. For those three weeks, I felt like myself, to the extent that any thirteen-year-old can really feel like herself. I loved living in the dorm, eating in the dining hall, doing homework late at night. I put up a *Simpsons* poster in my dorm room and made friends with three girls all coincidentally named Kristen who lived in my hall. I didn't want to leave.

When I got back to my old camp in August, it felt like someone had poured accelerant on everyone's social and sexual development. I was embarrassed that all that had happened between me and my nerd camp crush was a chaste slow dance, because Rachel and Co. were all getting fingered by their boyfriends on the soccer field after the stale cookies and Kool-Aid at evening snack. Soccer-field fingering didn't really appeal to me on a practical level (unsanitary, high probability of grass getting into your butt), but it nonetheless seemed like another rite of passage that I wasn't a part of. Each night, half the bunk would melt into the soccer field with the Seths and Joshes and Bens, and the other half—me, and the rest of the nonchosen—would silently make our way back to our bunk and wait for the rest of the girls to get back and tell us all about that night's adventures.

I hadn't even French-kissed anyone yet, which I hadn't been especially concerned with until now, when it suddenly seemed like I was *way* behind. So when, on the last night of camp that summer, the meanest girl in my bunk—a skinny, black-haired girl named Larissa whose pinched face and small eyes always looked like they were plotting something—came up to me and asked if I wanted to go to the basketball court to hook up with a guy our age named Steve, who was a friend of hers from home who was new at camp that summer, I said yes, even though I barely knew him and it seemed like there was a not-insignificant possibility that this was a trap. Would I get to the basketball court and wait there all night in vain while Larissa cackled at the success of her mean-girl plot? Steve wasn't one of the soccer-field boys, that much I knew, but beyond that we'd literally never said a word to each other.

I didn't ask Larissa, the madam of Bunk Thirteen, the obvious question: Had Steve requested *me*, or had he just charged Larissa with finding someone—*literally anyone*—to make out with that night, because it was the last night of camp and that was just what you did on the last night of camp. (It was 1990; apparently no one was concerned about the liability of dozens of horny kids wandering around unsupervised in the dead of night.)

Larissa and I walked over to the boys' area in silence. When we got there, the lights in most of the bunks, except for the ones belonging to the littlest kids, were on. We went into Steve's bunk; it was mostly empty, except for Steve. "You guys know each other, right?" Larissa said, gesturing to Steve. She didn't wait for an answer. "I gotta go," she said, and left.

Steve and I went to the basketball court and sat on the ground. There was barely any preamble before he leaned in and then his tongue was in my mouth and mine was in his. I closed my eyes—you were supposed to close your eyes, right? I was having trouble separating the act of kissing Steve from being aware of the act of kissing Steve. But as I walked back to the bunk, I couldn't help but smile, just a little. Now that I'd actually done it, I told myself it didn't matter if Steve had wanted to make out with me or not. It had *happened.* Now I wasn't a French-kissing virgin anymore.

I made out with a few more boys over the next year, including one who shoved his hands up my shirt while we watched the movie *Ghost* in a near-empty theater. But in high school, my self-consciousness took over, and I stood on the sidelines, figuratively and literally, when it came to relationships. I think I probably would have felt less alone if I'd actually bothered seeking out and talking to other people who were also not dating or having sex, but it was like I hated myself too much to admit that these were people I would find comfort with, and so I continued to seek out the approval and the treacherous friendship of the popular girls, because why would I join any club that would actually have me as a member? I identified with misfit smart-girl heroines like *My So-Called Life*'s Angela Chase and *Heathers*'s Veronica Sawyer, who left their former friends in the dust as they strived to be accepted by the popular clique, to sometimes disastrous results. It was the classic insecure smart-girl dilemma of desperately wanting to be accepted by the cool crowd, but also wanting to get good grades, and the two were almost never compatible. The only way to thread that needle was to do well in school while pretending that you didn't care if you did well, like you weren't working hard at it. But I *did* care, and it got increasingly harder to pretend that I didn't.

IN MY FAMILY, the misfit smart-girl persona stopped with me—if I was Veronica Sawyer, my sister Karen was Cher Horowitz, bubbly and blond (as though to drive this point home, she had all of *Clueless* memorized, seemingly the second it came out). The adorable baby grew into an adorable teenager who had an impossibly blond, tan, lacrosse-playing boyfriend in high school, as though he had been cut out from a *Popular Boys of High School* paper doll book. *She* had gotten that secret pink memo. I watched from afar in awe as she did exactly what she set out to do, whether it was winning a swimming championship or going straight to law school after college, and how people treated her like she was special. It seemed like, even at a young age, she never second-guessed herself.

But even though we were so different, as we grew older, we grew closer. By the time she got to law school, and I was at the *Observer,* we Gchatted almost every day. One day, over Gchat, she asked me if I thought it was "mandatory" to ask the groom's sisters to be in your bridal party when you got married, and I responded that I thought it was a sign of respect. She had started dating her boyfriend, Steve, earlier that year, but he lived in Washington, D.C., while she was still in law school in Miami.

> ME: Are you and Steve getting married?
> KAREN: Today? No.
> ME: Someday?
> KAREN: We shall see.

ME: !! Wowzers.

KAREN: You think I'd be doing this for nothing? All this travel and shit. Moving to D.C., etc.

ME: Damn girl! You're moving to D.C.?

KAREN: After graduation? Yeah, I mean if we are still together. You can't have a long-distance relationship forever. I'm not sure why this comes as a surprise.

ME: It's not really a "surprise"; it's more that you're 23!!

KAREN: Well, we aren't getting married tomorrow! And I turn 24 next week thank you very much!

ME: Ahahaha.

KAREN: I don't think 26 is too young to get engaged, married at 27.

Would you be shocked to learn that Karen did indeed get engaged at twenty-six and married at twenty-seven? I, for one, was not. (When we had this conversation, I was almost thirty-one, with no engagement or wedding in sight.) How foreign it felt to have your life figured out at such a young age, to be completely confident in your choices, to choose a profession where you would actually make money, to be perfectly content with the guy you'd started dating at twenty-three!

I had long told myself that we were so different, I wouldn't want her life. Being a lawyer sounded horribly boring; my life was so much more exciting. I had never seen myself as someone who cared much about hitting "adult" milestones at a certain point—it felt so *conventional*, didn't it? I was *not* conventional, I assured myself; if anything, I had always been a bit of a contrarian, taking pride in my ability to navigate the world on my own terms. I wasn't going to be someone who bookmarked engagement rings before they'd even met a partner or obsessed about climbing up the corporate ladder. I was proud of my position as someone always slightly out of sync with the mainstream—that was why, I thought, as a journalist, I was so good at skewering it.

But sometimes, I thought about my sister's life, and I wondered: What would it be like to move through the world in the way that she did, to be that comfortable in your own skin, to have a completely unwavering confidence in yourself? I could barely fathom it.

CHAPTER THREE

In contrast to my sister's direct line from high school to corporate law, my road to the *Observer*—and adulthood—had been circuitous. Starting in the fall of 2006, I'd been a writer for Gawker, a job I took after a summer of interning in the culture department at Slate, where I was a twenty-nine-year-old intern reporting to a twenty-five-year-old editorial assistant. I'd landed there after a patchwork of grad school and jobs: After a short stint in a PhD program in history (I dropped out after getting a master's degree), I got hired at a local paper, *Philadelphia Weekly*, as the arts and entertainment editor. Toward the end of my second year there, I started getting restless. I loved Philly, but it also felt like my career options there were limited. One day, while reading a popular media blog, I saw a small item about a new subject-based journalism program at Columbia University that was admitting students who already had some work experience, and they were going to be offering generous financial aid. Since I was still paying off undergraduate loans, I wasn't too stoked on the idea of taking on tens of thousands of dollars in additional loans, so this sounded perfect. That fall, I headed back to New York, where I'd lived for a year after graduating from college.

I wasn't sure what to expect from a new graduate program, especially since just a few years earlier, I had left graduate school. But now I was twenty-eight, I thought. Older and wiser. Still, at the end of the program, I didn't have a job. I did, however, have an offer to be an intern at Slate, for $15 an hour. So now I was twenty-nine, and an intern—a paid intern, but still an intern. Maybe I shouldn't have left Philly, I thought. I could still be working as the arts and entertainment editor at *Philadelphia Weekly*, drinking too much at the 700 Club, going to sweaty shows at the Khyber. It wasn't a bad life at all.

Was I just someone who was never satisfied with whatever she was doing? That was a grim thought. I didn't want to be that person, but it was true that I did tire of things quickly. I'd never stayed at a job for more than two years; since breaking up with Jake, my college boyfriend, when I was twenty-four, I hadn't dated anyone for longer than a year and a half. Or maybe this was just a part of growing up—trying things out and knowing enough about yourself to cut bait when it was clear it wasn't going well. But if that was true, how long was this stage of trying things on for size going to last?

In the meantime, the summer—and my internship at Slate—was nearing its end. One day I was sitting in an editorial meeting when the TV critic had an idea. "Chuck Klosterman has a new book coming out," he said. "Has anyone ever noticed that his author photos are *ridiculous*? Like each one is just more pretentious than the next. We should do an analysis of Chuck Klosterman's author photos." Everyone laughed.

"Great idea," said the editor in chief.

"That's so funny," another editor agreed.

"Doree, you should write it," the TV critic said.

"Um, okay, sure," I said. I was flattered that he had thought of me for the piece, and it seemed like something that I could run with and be funny, something that was a little outside of Slate's generally self-serious articles and essays. I'd never actually read any of Chuck Klosterman's books, but that, apparently, did not matter.

The piece I wrote was pretty mean-spirited, and it didn't dawn on me until much later that I'd been used—no one who was actually on staff wanted to put their name on an article trashing Chuck Klosterman, and I was too naïve to realize it. But the piece caught the eye of a couple of editors at Gawker, and they hired me as an associate editor, along with Emily Gould, a former publishing assistant with a pointedly funny blog, who was a few years younger than me. My boss for most of my time at Gawker was Choire Sicha, who had been the second-ever editor of the site and had been lured back to run it by Gawker founder and overlord Nick Denton.

Denton sometimes seemed like a cartoonish supervillain. He was a forty-year-old Brit, very tall, with an enormous head but kind of pinched face, and closely cropped hair. After making millions selling an early internet business, he had moved to New York and launched the gadget blog Gizmodo in 2002 and followed it a few months later with Gawker. Over the course of four years, he had built it into a small network of other blogs. He was one of those bosses who would get completely fixated on one part of his company, and then suddenly move on to something else. But when you were in his sights, he was unrelenting. He deeply enjoyed tweaking the media establishment, and he had certain obsessions—the short-lived

Condé Nast business magazine *Portfolio* being one of them, the micro-celebrity Julia Allison being another—that he insisted we cover constantly.

Denton seemed to relish keeping his employees scared. We rarely heard from him directly; he communicated all his opinions about our work through Chris, my first boss at Gawker, and later Choire. When Denton was in the office—a storefront* on Crosby Street in SoHo, a block or so away from the luxury condominium building where he lived—a chill went through the room. It felt like he could sneak up behind you at any time and rip whatever you were doing to shreds. His attitude about almost everything was sneering, judgmental, caustic, and that was the posture we were expected to take with whatever we wrote about.

At first, I actually found this perspective refreshing. We were speaking truth to power! We were exposing hypocrisy! We were the scrappy underdogs who picked our targets carefully and exposed them for what they really were! And it was fun to write in a snide, snarky tone, to act like we knew better than everyone else reading. I especially loved when I managed to get into places or parties I wasn't supposed to, like a book party for the author Christopher Hitchens that was held in the ridiculously over-the-top Upper East Side apartment of a Republican megadonor who had a photo album devoted to her dog's trips to France on display in the library. I loved these little glimpses into a completely unfamiliar, but fascinating, world.

---

* The office was also next door to the unmarked door leading to a basement counterfeit handbags operation, so there were always groups of confused tourists peering through our windows wondering if this was where they could get their fake Louis Vuitton Carryalls.

But Gawker also played to my worst instincts, as though Harriet the Spy had been given permission to just run with everything mean she wrote in her notebook. Being mean, day in and day out, started to wear on me—I didn't like that my default take on everything had to be so worthy of scorn. And when I stopped to think about it, just what *was* I doing at Gawker? Was my purpose in life cranking out multiple mocking blog posts a day?

After a few months, I was tiring of the constant churn, and I was also tiring of the default stance that I had to take with each post—the assumption was that everyone and everything we wrote about was deserving of mockery. There was no room for empathy, no room for nuance. The point of view that I'd initially found alluring and fun was becoming altogether depressing. Was *everyone* an incompetent hypocrite? Certainly *many* wealthy people in positions of power are, in fact, incompetent hypocrites, but I started to feel like sometimes I was punching down. Should I care about an article that some underpaid assistant editor wrote in a lifestyle magazine just to mock it? Did it matter that the Park Slope Parents Listserv was up in arms about the gender of a hat? We writers were egged on by the site's commenters, a crew of people who seemed to spend just as much time as we did on the internet, if not more, but who also were quick to turn on us if they felt we hadn't upheld the covenant of the site. It was a vicious cycle, where we felt we were performing for an audience of mostly anonymous commenters, but who we also treated with some degree of scorn. After all, at least we were getting paid to be snarky on the internet; they were doing it for free.

Denton encouraged us to turn people into characters, particularly anyone who had even the smallest desire for fame, and write about them repeatedly and relentlessly. When I stopped to think about it, I was sometimes a little worried about how easy I found it to be mean. But meanness was rewarded—by traffic, by commenters, by Choire and Denton.

So when Peter Kaplan emailed me a couple of months later, it felt not just like my dream editor had noticed me, but I was getting a lifeline, a way out of the digital sweatshop. And now, just two years later, it had been taken away.

AFTER THE LAYOFF, I tried to put on a brave face. I wrote posts on my Tumblr about all the things I was doing with my "fun-employment"; I made a big show of getting together with other laid-off and freelance friends during the day, just because I could. But really, I was deeply hurt. I'd never been laid off before, and it made me second-guess everything. Like: Were there things I could have done differently at work? Did I act too entitled? Did I not make friends with the right people? If I'd made more of an effort with Tom, would he have kept me on? Had I thought of myself as above office politics, or had I just woefully misread the politics of the office? Or maybe it wasn't about office politics at all; maybe I just wasn't a good enough writer or reporter to stay on. Or maybe I was too expensive, since I was one of the better-paid reporters in the newsroom. Should I have asked for less money when I got hired? These questions replayed in my mind on a loop, as I sat at my desk in my apartment sending out free-lance pitches. I was having trouble believing that I would ever work again.

The day I'd gotten laid off, my friends Alison and Melissa, who were also writers, had informed me that they were taking me out for drinks that night at a bar we liked in Tribeca to drown my sorrows in alcohol.

"They suck," Alison said matter-of-factly, referring to the *Observer.*

"*Seriously,*" Melissa said.

"What if I never get another job?" I asked.

"You'll get another job," Alison said. "I know you will." I wasn't sure I believed her, but it didn't matter. In that moment, I just needed a friend who really got me to tell me everything was going to be okay.

Alison, especially, was that friend. We'd met when I worked for *Philadelphia Weekly* and had been roommates briefly. People often said we looked like sisters, or at least, cousins, although I think people saw two white women with shoulder-length brown hair and the kinds of similar mannerisms and inside jokes that come with years of friendship and thought we looked more alike than we actually did.

Like me, my close friends in New York mostly worked in media. Alison and Melissa were both bloggers, and then there was Tess, a newspaper editor; Lara, an art director at a Condé Nast magazine; Emily, whom I'd worked with at Gawker; Rebecca, an editor at Hearst; and Gabrielle, who also worked at Condé Nast. We were all in our late twenties or early thirties, not at the top of a masthead but not at the bottom, either, and none of us had kids yet. We were one another's support systems, a place to vent when our bosses were being especially infuriating, when we got edits that made no sense, when we felt like we worked twice as hard as the men in our department for less recognition. (Most of us worked for men.) But we also celebrated one another's promotions and new jobs and cover stories. I was grateful to have these women in my life.

CHAPTER FOUR

In my twenties, I had a tendency to fall into relationships without thinking too hard. I didn't "date," exactly; if I met someone, and we hung out, and made out or slept together, we usually ended up calling each other boyfriend and girlfriend. But I'd been a late bloomer in the relationships department. At college, surrounded by people who were always coupling off, and a Greek system that seemed to exist mostly so that people could hook up, I saw myself as a sad, lonely, unattractive outcast when it came to guys. I'd always had plenty of female friends, but I was so scared of rejection that I was reluctant to ever tell guys how I felt about them. Instead, I developed deep, unrequited crushes and never said anything, hoping that one day a lightbulb would go off in the brain of the object of my affection and they would realize, in perfect eighties teen movie fashion, that *the right one had been there all along* (the right one was, of course, me).

I knew these were just Hollywood fantasies, but because I'd never been in an actual relationship, they were my only frame of reference. In the movies, the awkward girl or the tomboy or the outcast always ended up, miraculously, with the boy of her dreams. Surely *someone* would be able to pierce the armor I'd put up for myself and sweep me off my feet? It didn't seem *that* far-fetched, but then again, I also had no idea what being in a relationship really entailed. It was like being so focused on the wedding that you forget that you have to actually be married afterward—I was so obsessed with the idea of "getting a boy-friend" that I had no concept of what happened next.

I coped by becoming friends with my crushes. I could be the cool girl friend (but not the cool *girlfriend*), the confi-dante. If I couldn't date them, then at least I could be in close proximity to them. But this could also be incredibly painful, and sometimes, it seemed like I was just setting myself up for more heartache. In college, instead of trying to get distance from my freshman crush, I agreed to live in a big off-campus house with him and six other people my sophomore year. When he promptly started dating one of our other roommates—my friend—I played it cool, as though I didn't care at all, like I was *totally* over him. But actually, it sucked.

I threw myself into my classes, double majoring in history and English and doing a minor in art history, and got involved in the school paper, where in the second semester of my soph-omore year I became editor of the weekly arts and entertain-ment magazine. And I loved my motley crew of friends—at a school dominated by a Greek system, we were proudly, almost pretentiously outside of it. There was Daniel, an impossibly tall, impossibly handsome gay guy who'd been raised Ortho-dox Jewish; we bonded over our mutual love of Pavement and modern architecture, but also loved driving around Philly in his Saab (christened "Miss Saab") blasting the Spice Girls. Jill was my first friend at school—we met in our economics class our freshman year and were both from the Boston area—and I was drawn to her Uma-Thurman-in-*Pulp-Fiction* haircut and obsession with Italy. I'd met Meera during our freshman orientation, playing Human Bingo in the quad; she complimented my turquoise nail polish and I complimented her patent-leather dog collar necklace. Senior year, Jill, Meera, and I lived with another friend, Liz, a chemistry major from Connecticut with whom I'd gone to dozens of concerts in Philly and New York. The four of us threw parties featuring our friends' bands, cooked dinner together, and watched *The X-Files*. Down the block, Daniel hosted hours-long Shabbat dinners at his apartment that ended in impromptu dance parties. I had found my people, and I had resigned myself to the idea that a romantic relationship just might not be in the cards for me—not now, maybe not ever. Sex remained a foreign concept, something that everyone else seemed to instinctively understand how to make happen for themselves and that I just didn't.

Then, during the second semester of my senior year, when I was twenty-one, I met Jake. He was a skinny, unassumingly cute guy with dark hair who wore corduroys and glasses. We were both English majors; we both listened to Belle and Sebastian; we both happened to be going to New York over spring break. We rode up together on New Jersey Transit and didn't stop talking and made plans to hang out the next night. At Max Fish, the bar on the Lower East Side, we kissed for the first time. Was this it? I wondered. Was I finally going to have a boyfriend? When we got back to school after break, we started hanging out more, and it felt *easy*. He liked me, and I liked him, and that was it. After so much time being single and feeling like love would never happen for me, it felt surreal to then be completely enamored with someone and want to see them all the time, cook dinner with them, go to movies with them, sleep in and skip class with them.

Jake was also moving to New York after we graduated, to live at his aunt and uncle's in Greenwich Village, and we fit seamlessly into each other's lives. Instead of just me, it was now Jake and Doree. Doree and Jake. He moved out of his aunt and uncle's apartment and into his own place in Park Slope, and I liked the weekend routines that we settled into: bagels from the place down the block, the Sunday paper, meet-ups with friends at the park or a bar. But then I went back to Philly for a graduate program in history, and even though I came up to New York as soon as my classes ended each week, it wasn't the same. We were drifting apart. We broke up when I was twenty-four. And then, with exactly one real relationship under my belt, I felt like I needed to make up for lost time. I became a serial monogamist.

In the span of five years, while living in Philadelphia, I had long-term relationships with: an optician I met while I was buying glasses, a union organizer, a newspaper editor, and an art student who smoked pot every day. I was attracted to all of them, I even loved a couple of them, but it also felt like I was trying on different identities and different life paths through the guys I was dating. I didn't see it that way at the time, and I didn't consider my boyfriends to be anthropological studies, but the novelty of each one was invigorating; in a way, the ephemerality was the point. I didn't know exactly who I was yet, or what I really wanted from a relationship or a partner— I only knew what they expected me to be, and it was exciting, for a time, to try to be those people.

· · ·

I MET JON the summer after I graduated from Columbia through his older brother, who was good friends with some college friends—including, somewhat awkwardly, Jake. Jon was a tall, bespectacled man with reddish hair who, unlike anyone else I knew, worked in New York State government as the chief of staff for a state senator. In my world, this counted as exotic; it gave him a vaguely do-gooder sheen that was appealing. He knew all the acronyms of state and city agencies *and* what they did!

Jon and I started flirting over Myspace, because in the fall of 2006 that was still where you flirted with your crushes on social media. Facebook was still mostly for people in college— I only had an account because we had been instructed to sign up for one at Columbia, although I almost never looked at it—and I barely knew what Twitter was. So leaving puns and funny photos on someone's Myspace "wall" was a good way to signal your interest. Finally, I texted Jon one night asking if he wanted to go to an indie rock show at Mercury Lounge. I figured I didn't have much to lose, and if he said no or didn't respond, I could always just plausibly say that I was asking him to go as friends. Because we *were* friends, right? He responded that he was out of town, but could we hang out when he got back? We could.

We quickly started the rituals of early relationship life: I met his college friends, he took me to work events, we had sex at night *and* in the morning. And almost from the time we started dating, Jon and I went to a lot of weddings. Like, a *lot* of weddings. He was three years younger than me, twenty-six to my twenty-nine when we first met, and so we were both at that age when it seems like half your disposable income is going to weddings, and wedding gifts, and bachelor parties, and he had gone to a small liberal arts college where a lot of people had started dating in college and stayed together and got married at the stroke of twenty-seven. We went to a wedding in California of a family friend of his and afterward drove up the coast in a convertible. In Big Sur, we stayed in a small cabin and hiked to a waterfall and ate pancakes in a tiny treetop restaurant; we visited Hearst Castle and gaped at the opulence. It felt like I had met someone who wasn't just trustworthy and dependable, but someone fun and adventurous. For the first time, it really felt like my boyfriend and I were a *team.*

We moved in together after a year. I started at the *Observer* and he got a new job, working for a more prominent New York politician. "Power couple!" Alison said.

I scoffed. "Hardly." I knew that it was uncool to say you were in a power couple, but I was secretly a little pleased that she had called us that. It was my first experience dating someone who had a job that (at least from the outside) seemed prestigious, and it felt good to tell people who Jon worked for.

But even though Jon's job *sounded* prestigious, he was miserable—the stress of it had caused him to develop severe heartburn, and he had to go on a restricted diet. And then, a year later, when I lost my job at the *Observer,* my career wasn't the only aspect of my life that I was starting to question. My relationship with Jon had been cruising along on autopilot for at least the last year. We had gone through all the motions of a couple who were in this for the long haul: Our parents had met, he had bonded with my dog, we started talking about buying an apartment together, we watched *30 Rock* together on the couch. (I know—we were basically living a young white Brooklyn couple cliché.) I liked his friends and he liked mine. We went on vacation and out to dinner and to parties. We were a *unit*. We had been together long enough, and were old enough, that getting married was a logical next step.

But we weren't engaged, and the weddings we went to together were becoming not as much fun as they used to be. I started to dread sitting next to Jon as we watched couple after couple say "I do," as he and I avoided eye contact, with the unspoken fact of our nonengagedness hanging over our heads. I was now thirty-one. I had never lived with anyone I was in a relationship with before Jon, because I had told myself that I would only live with someone who I could see marrying. An engagement didn't have to be an ultimatum to move in together, but I also felt like I needed to at least have that commitment to myself that this was a relationship I was taking seriously. And yet, there was no engagement, and it made me question not just Jon's commitment to me, but mine to Jon.

At coffee with Daniel, I tried to unknot this increasingly thorny problem. "I can't tell if I want to get engaged because I want to marry Jon, or if I just want to get married, period," I said. Daniel had recently moved in with a new boyfriend, and I thought they would probably get married.

"Hmm," he said. "I mean, there would be a lot worse things than getting married to Jon, right?"

"That's not particularly enthusiastic," I said. "Like, 'it could be worse' doesn't really scream 'till death do us part.'" I took a sip of coffee and contemplated this. "I don't know, maybe you're right. But it doesn't seem like he wants to get married to me."

"Well, he does," Daniel said authoritatively. "He's just young. Give him some time."

But our conversations about getting engaged went in circles. "I *do* want to get married," Jon told me not long after we had moved into a new rental apartment in Carroll Gardens, another Brooklyn neighborhood a couple of miles south of our old place in Fort Greene. The apartment was much bigger, probably twice the size of our old place, with very high ceilings and great closet space and a *dishwasher* (the New York apartment holy grail). It felt like a new start, moving into an apartment that was *ours,* not mine that Jon had moved into, and yet, we still had not resolved when or whether we were going to get engaged. He had told me that there was a large diamond in his family that, when the time came, he would be able to cut and make into a ring for me. "But I don't feel ready. I need to get my career to a better place. I need to make more money." This struck me as a cop-out; Jon's family was well-off, and he'd mentioned the trust fund he would inherit at thirty-five enough times to make me think that money would never *really* be an issue for him. It also raised some uncomfortable questions for me about whether we were in an equal partnership. I didn't feel like Jon needed to make more money before we got married, but if *he* did, then maybe we weren't on the same page about money—or anything else.

"When do you think you'll feel ready?" I asked quietly. I suddenly felt like I might cry. I was fully aware that I was living out a horrible relationship cliché—the woman who's desperate to get married, the man who is resisting but not resisting enough that he wants to break up. But even as I said it, I wondered if I really wanted to get married to Jon, or if I just didn't want to feel like a horrible relationship cliché. I realized, with a sinking feeling, that I had started viewing our relationship transactionally: I had put in the time and the effort, and so there should be an engagement at the end of it—which of course is very different than feeling like you're getting engaged to someone you're deeply in love with, who's just as excited about you as you are about them, that this is just the beginning of a long life together. I had lost track of the love and excitement; the engagement was feeling more like an end, not a beginning.

"I don't know," he said.

A few weeks later, I was at a friend's birthday party at a bar in my neighborhood. Jon wasn't with me, and I started talking with one of my former Gawker co-workers, Alex. He asked how Jon was. "He's fine," I said. I paused. I had had a couple of drinks already and was feeling loquacious. "I'm just at the point, you know, where I'm not sure if I should wait around for him to be ready to get married or if I should sort of cut my losses and just break up with him now, because who knows how long that will take," I said quickly. It wasn't the sort of thing I'd normally just blurt out, but I knew Alex would be honest with me.

"How old are you?" he asked.

I had just turned thirty-two, I told him.

"Do you want kids?"

"Yeah. I mean, I think so?" I said.

"So, okay, say you and Jon break up," he said. "Even if you started dating someone right away, it'd probably be at least, what, two years before you got engaged? And another year until you got married, and then maybe another year before you had a kid? So now you're thirty-six." He paused. "I feel like, unless things are *really* bad, that you should just stick it out with Jon."

To see it laid out so starkly like that was sobering. *Thirty-six!* Even though it was only four years away, it felt *so old.* Until that moment, I hadn't *thought* that I believed that women were washed-up, dating-wise, at thirty-five. But maybe I *had* in fact absorbed the messages that came from everywhere about women's expiration dates, and I didn't feel strong enough to confront my own internalized misogyny. Alex was right— I *should* stick it out with Jon. Worst case was that he'd come around in, what, a year—right? I could wait that long.

The alternative seemed grim, but I was also embarrassed that I thought the alternative was grim. I *was* a progressive feminist—or at least I thought I was. But then why was I so fixated on getting engaged and married and having kids? It felt like it was the logical next step, but *why*? Was it my parents? They had never overtly pressured me, but they made it clear that they were expecting that Jon and I would be engaged soon—but maybe that was because I had telegraphed that we would be engaged soon. Was it my "biological clock"? Maybe, although I also had faith in the medical establishment to assist in that department if necessary. Was it the couples we were friends with who had been together for around the same amount of time who had recently gotten engaged? I didn't want to admit it, but I felt a little bit of competitiveness and jealousy. Why was it happening for them, and not for us?

Hanging over all of these questions was a big, uncomfortable one: Was there something wrong with me? Was I someone that men wanted to date but not marry, and if not, then why not? The situation with Jon surfaced all of my old insecurities; I was convinced that the problem lay with me, with some vibe I emitted, something that told guys, *Mmm, she's nothing special, maybe try the next one.*

Meanwhile, Jon's older brother Eric had a reputation as a commitment-phobic bachelor, but he had started dating someone seriously, and after less than a year, they were engaged. This threw me for a loop. Jon and I were supposed to be the couple who got engaged! *Eric* was supposed to be the bachelor!

One weekend, not long after Eric and his fiancée, Nicole, had gotten engaged, the four of us drove up to Eric and Jon's parents' house to celebrate their father's sixtieth birthday. They lived in a quaint seaside town in southern Massachusetts, the weather was perfect, and I was going to wear a new silk Rachel Comey dress with oysters on it that I had spent way too much money on at one of those Brooklyn boutiques where you know you can't really afford anything, but then you walk in and you get seduced by the sight of one perfect row of clogs and beautiful leather bags and simple, elegant dresses, and when I had tried on this dress, I had instantly felt cool and beautiful and next thing I knew I was taking out my credit card and it was mine.

But when I got to Jon's parents' house, even the dress couldn't mask my dejection at my situation. The afternoon of the party, while everyone else in his family was downstairs, waiting for guests to arrive, I couldn't bear to leave the bedroom we were staying in. Finally, Jon came up to see what was wrong.

I burst into tears. "I . . . just . . . can't . . . handle . . . that . . . Eric . . . and . . . Nicole . . . are . . . already . . . engaged!" I said, hyperventilating through tears.

Jon seemed uncomfortable. "I'm sorry," he said. He paused. "Do you want to come downstairs? Everyone's wondering where you are."

Jon's ambivalence hurt. It made me question just how much he loved me, and how much he felt committed. My logic went like this: If he loved me like he said he did, and he wanted to make me happy, then why did he persist in making me so miserable? To me, his excuses about why we weren't engaged yet rang hollow. People did the things they really wanted to do. If Jon *really* wanted to get married to me, it wouldn't matter if we had no money at all. Plenty of people got engaged when their careers were in flux, their financial status shaky. His refusal to get engaged felt like a daily rejection of *me*.

But I was also angry at myself because I wasn't *supposed* to be the kind of person who would be so upset about not getting engaged that I was sobbing on a floral bedspread at my presumptive in-laws' house. I wasn't an engagement ring Pinterest board person! Being so upset about not being engaged challenged the self-image I had of myself as cool, sophisticated, feminist, and certainly *not* part of any aspect of the mainstream wedding industrial complex. What did it say about me, now, that I was?

I remembered how lonely I felt in college, when it seemed like everyone around me was partnering up, and I was the only one who didn't have a boyfriend, or even just having sex with someone. Now, I knew, I *liked* being in a relationship; I liked being in love. I also had no road map for what a life without a partner really looked like. Even as women's media preached messages of empowerment, so much of it was laser focused on finding (and keeping) a partner. I didn't have any older single friends I could turn to for advice, or just to hear that it would be okay. My mom's one single female friend was a TV writer about whom my mom always spoke with pity. She didn't have to say the message that I heard loud and clear: In her youth, this friend had been too picky, too focused on her creative career, and *look where that got her* (besides an Emmy). In my mom's telling, this friend had long been miserable *because* she was single; the fact of her singledom had overshadowed everything else she had done in her life. According to my mother, this friend would often tell my mom how lucky she was to be married and have children. Even now, in her sixties, she was, supposedly, still trying to find a man. I didn't want to turn into her, but I also never thought to question my mom's perception of her friend. I was scared of interrogating a world in which an accomplished, brilliant, hilarious woman felt that her entire life had been a waste because she had never gotten married.

When we got back to Brooklyn, it became clear that my relationship with Jon was slowly dissolving, and I was doing nothing to stop it, but also nothing to accelerate its demise. I didn't want to admit defeat. Everything with Jon culminated in a miserable Memorial Day weekend trip to Nova Scotia with friends of ours, another couple who also seemed like they hated each other.

We were barely speaking when we got back from the trip. A few days later, I met up with my friend Jenna for oysters and we discussed our respective relationships; she was also in the midst of figuring out whether she was going to break up with her long-term boyfriend. "I think I'm going to move out," she said.

"Whoa," I said. "So you're gonna do it."

"Yeah," she said. "What about you? How are you feeling about everything?"

"Ugh," I said. "I can, like, see it dissolving before my eyes, but I feel totally frozen about doing anything about it. And he's so passive that he would never break up with me."

"You should do it," she said. "I'm going to start looking at apartments."

An idea occurred to me. "Do you . . . want a roommate?"

Her eyes lit up. "That would be so fun! Let's look at some apartments!"

It felt good to have a plan. I didn't feel bad that Jon had no idea what I was planning, but I also told myself that he had to at least have an inkling about what was going on. We were essentially living separate lives at this point; I went out with friends almost every night, and he rarely came with me. Jenna and I looked at a couple of apartments together, but nothing felt right, and eventually we decided to look at places on our own. I found a sublet on Craigslist back in Fort Greene, just a couple of blocks away from my old apartment. It seemed perfect: a garden apartment in a brownstone, and I could bring my dog.

Finally, I told Jon I was moving out. "Where are you going?" he asked. He seemed blindsided—not necessarily by the fact that I wanted to break up, but that I had already set things in motion without him. I felt a little bad—had it been deceptive of me to do all this behind his back?—but ultimately rationalized that I needed the plan in place to have the breakup conversation in the first place.

"I found a sublet in Fort Greene," I said. "Lee is going to come with me." Lee had originally been my dog, but for the past three and a half years had felt like *our* dog. Jon looked sad when I said that, and it occurred to me that he was probably more upset about losing the dog than losing me. "I think we can evaluate our options when the summer is over," I said, as though I were an HR manager having a conversation with an underperforming employee. It dawned on me that it was possible he wasn't blindsided by the fact that we were separating, but because I was moving out and wasn't asking *him* to be the one to move out. But I knew I had to be the one to leave him, and the apartment. There would just be too many memories of him, and of us, if I stayed.

He nodded. I don't think even I believed that we would be "evaluating our options" when the summer was over, just as I doubt any employee in the history of corporate America has been put on a Performance Improvement Plan and not eventually been fired. It was just a way to ease us both out of the situation, but I almost immediately regretted not just ripping the Band-Aid off. It was clear that we both knew that this was the end. And even though I'd technically broken up with Jon, I felt like he had led me there but was ultimately too scared or lazy to break up with me himself, which made me hate him in that way where you don't even want to expend the energy to actually hate someone but suddenly things have come into focus so clearly that you're simultaneously disgusted with him and yourself.

Nothing had ever been *bad,* exactly, in our relationship; it had just been a long time since things had been *good,* and those kinds of relationships are the hardest to extricate yourself from. And yet, nothing was ever really great between us—it was fine, and for a long time fine was enough. Until, of course, it wasn't.

CHAPTER FIVE

I brought very little to the sublet. Jon had kept the bed in our old place, so I ordered a new bed frame and mattress on Overstock, and, on the beautiful marble fireplace mantel in the bedroom of the new apartment, lined up the books that I'd brought with me, my "these are the ones I'm saving in the fire" books like *Harriet the Spy* and *The Believers* and *The Intuitionist* and *Heartburn,* the novelization of Nora Ephron and Carl Bernstein's divorce, which was admittedly a little on the nose. I folded the suitcase's worth of summer clothes and put them on the shelf in the closet. The apartment felt refreshingly spare—none of Jon's dirty socks on the bedroom floor, no unread mail cluttering the entryway table, no shaving products taking up valuable bathroom sink real estate. My newfound minimalism was calming, even as I sometimes missed the four huge bookcases and overstuffed dresser in the old place.

But sprinkled in with the calmness was the unnerving feeling that I was moving backward. I was thirty-three, getting to the point where—even in New York where it can seem like people stay single forever—my friends who were married or engaged were starting to outnumber those who weren't. I didn't regret my decision to break things off with Jon, but I did have the creeping feeling that perhaps what I had thought would be forward momentum was actually putting me back in time, to a period in my twenties when I lived alone and was single, with just Lee to keep me company.

In the weeks after I moved out, I started losing weight—not deliberately, exactly, but now that I was living alone, I wasn't eating at restaurants as much, and sometimes I would forget to eat lunch, or just grab something quickly at the coffee shop around the corner. But once I started noticing that my clothes were looser, I found it hard to stop. I started weighing myself every day and charting my "progress" on an app, and I got great satisfaction at watching the chart of my weight go down, down, and down some more, and the positive reinforcement I got from everyone around me—"You look *amazing!*"—just fueled my desire to get smaller. My whole life, I'd been told "beauty comes from within," but even though I'd always known deep down that that was a lie, to see the world reinforcing and rewarding a very specific version of external beauty was eye-opening. It was like I had finally gotten the pink memo, and it turned out that, yes, of *course* I was treated better because of how I looked. It was intoxicating, but also scary, like a kid who'd been given the keys to a brand-new car the second she got her learner's permit. I worried that I, too, would crash.

I had never been the pretty girl, and historically I had taken a sort of refuge in this identity. It was comfortable, familiar. Even once I started dating, I told myself that I wasn't beautiful—cute, maybe, but I reasoned that guys who were into me probably liked my personality, not my totally average looks. It was armor to shield me from what I was convinced would be the inevitable rejection from anyone I was remotely interested in, a self-loathing comfort zone that got reinforced over and over again, usually because I was too chicken to ever tell people how I felt about them. And yet, I paradoxically came across as incredibly self-assured and confident, even if that was never how I saw myself. I always felt crushingly insecure and worried not just about what people thought of me, but whether they would include me; I had a near-pathological fear of being left out, of feeling like I wasn't in on the joke, that I didn't get the memo. At camp the summer I was twelve my quote for the summer on the bunk plaque was, "What about me?" When I protested, the girl who had been in charge of the plaque—a bottle blonde whose boyfriend had snuck into our bunk at least three times a week so they could make out on the creaky metal bunk beds— shrugged and said, "I mean, you *do* say that a lot."

ONE NIGHT IN college, my friend Will and I were sitting on the floor of the school newspaper building's lobby, waiting for the shuttle to pick us up. We both worked for the weekly arts and entertainment magazine, and it had been a long night getting the magazine ready for publication. I was exhausted.

"So you know that I'm in love with you, right?" he said suddenly.

"Um . . ." I said. I had thought that it was *possible* that Will had a crush on me, but I was so used to being the crusher, not the crushee, that I had put it out of my mind. It was barely comprehensible to me that someone could find me attractive, let alone be *in love* with me.

"Well, I am," he said. "I'm not expecting anything from you. I just thought you should know."

"Okay," I said. I didn't feel the same way—I liked Will as a friend, and I thought he was a brilliant writer and a kind person, but I was not in love with him. I was also a little bit repulsed—not because he was repulsive, but because if Will loved me, then he *had* to be a loser, right? Only a disgusting loser would be in love with *me*. I realized that he must have hoped that I would respond differently, that declaring his love for me must have taken courage that he wasn't sure he possessed. I knew this because I was usually the person who was pining after their friend, and most of the time, I pined in silence. Will was showing me, I thought, what the guys I pined after thought about me: sweet, well-meaning, but ultimately deserving of pity, and certainly not someone to be in a relationship with.

Now, more than ten years later, I felt like I finally had the sexual power that had always eluded me. But it was dangerous, addictive. The validation that I got when someone found me attractive was a dopamine rush, and when men responded to it, it just fueled my need for more validation from them. I was going out almost every night, drinking until I got drunk, flirting, and feeling omnipotent.

One of the guys I fixated on was Max, someone I'd met through friends who was almost impossibly hot and alluringly aloof. We slept together, and then when he started ignoring me I flirted with Tim, a bartender at the bar down the street from my apartment, who Max was friendly with. I had a fantasy that this would make Max jealous (it didn't). One summer night, after hours of hanging out at the bar where Tim worked, we went back to my place.

Tim wandered over to the fireplace and stared at the mantel. "You have *so many* books," he said, sounding both impressed and confused. "You must like to read!"

"Um . . . yeah, I do," I said. I saw him a couple more times, but his comment stuck in my head. Even if he was just a fling, I couldn't bring myself to sleep with someone who thought that fifteen books in your apartment was a lot.

AT THE END of the summer, Jon and I got together for a drink. We hadn't seen each other since I'd told him I was leaving. "So . . . I don't think we should get back together," I said.

He nodded. "Yeah, I figured." We sat in silence for a moment. Our relationship was going out not with a bang, but a whimper. There was a part of me that wished it had been more dramatic. Why hadn't Jon fought for me, or even registered any objections to ending the relationship?

"I can come by and get the rest of my stuff in a couple of days, if that works?" I quickly added, "I can come while you're at work."

"Yeah," he said. "That's fine." We didn't do a postmortem of our relationship, or discuss anything else about the breakup. We finished our drinks and left. It was an appropriately anticlimactic end to a relationship that had sputtered to its conclusion. I told myself that this was a mature way to break up, not a depressing, emotionless ending to spending nearly four years of my life with someone.

But now, my sublet was ending, so I had to officially start my new life. I found a cute apartment on Craigslist that was just a few blocks away; it was occupied by a couple who were leaving New York and looking for someone to take over their lease. It was perfect: on the second floor of a small apartment building, with a decent-sized living room with a big window overlooking a picturesque block of Fort Greene, a new kitchen,

a small, quiet bedroom. Hardwood floors! *I will be happy here,*
I thought.

When I went back to the old apartment to get the rest of
my things, it felt like walking into a time capsule, even though
it had been only three months. The traces of past-me were
everywhere—my favorite posters on the walls, clothes hanging
in the closet, books on the shelves, even toiletries still in the
bathroom. The thought crossed my mind that it wasn't too late
to slip back into my old life, tell Jon that I wanted to give
things another shot. I could stop fixating on getting engaged
and try to repair what had gone wrong. But as I started going
through my stuff, deciding what to keep and what to take with
me, I was overcome by deep sadness. What had been the point?
I wondered. Why did *anyone* allow themselves to even *try* to
build a life with someone, if it was just going to end with a
Man With A Van, boxes of discarded books left in the lobby,
and the feeling that you'd just wasted almost four years of your
life?

On the dresser in the bedroom, I saw a lease that Jon
had signed for an apartment nearby. I felt simultaneously
indignant—how *dare* he move on so quickly!—but also, relieved. Thank *God* he was moving on so quickly. It absolved
me of any guilt about the breakup, I told myself, or how I'd
handled it.

CHAPTER SIX

A few weeks after I moved into my new apartment, it was the week of the annual CMJ event in New York, a music festival that showcased up-and-coming bands at various venues around the city, and my friend Claire, who worked for a music marketing agency, had invited me out to see some shows. We started the night at a small party at a bar on the Lower East Side, then she got a text from a co-worker that he was at Bowery Ballroom, a venue on Delancey Street that wasn't too far, so we headed over there.

I was feeling confident—hot, even—and a little tipsy, but not *too* drunk, just the right amount of drunk where things seem possible. I was wearing a skintight Mackage leather jacket that I'd bought at the Bloomingdale's in SoHo a few days earlier. It had cost a fortune, four hundred dollars. I couldn't afford it, but I'd bought it anyway: I'd been ghosted by a guy I'd gone out with a few times whom I had developed some budding, "this could turn into something" feelings for. He, apparently, did not feel the same way. Even if I never saw him again, I wanted to make sure I looked good if I *did* happen to run into him—so good that he would rue the day he hadn't returned my texts. I called it my revenge jacket. I felt sexy and powerful and badass in it—*definitely* not like someone who would get ghosted. Revenge Jacket Doree behaved differently than I did. She was fun! And spontaneous! And a little bit wild! She for *sure* didn't overthink things. She was always up for whatever; she was the life of the party. She was someone I had never been, never thought I could be, and now somehow, sort of, was. I simultaneously loved and hated her.

When we got to Bowery Ballroom, we found Claire's co-worker. He was with a friend, a blond hipsterish guy visiting from North Carolina. The friend seemed a little bland, but cute—and wide-eyed, like this was his first time in the Big City. We started talking, and then, as the electropop performer DOM took the stage, we were making out, and the next thing I knew we were on the subway going back to my apartment.

"What do you do, anyway?" I asked as we snuggled on the F train. I was trying to pay attention so we wouldn't miss my transfer, but this spontaneous, unexpected encounter was exciting. I realized I knew basically nothing about this guy, except that he was a friend of a co-worker of a friend—vetted, but barely.

"I'm a Breathalyzer salesman," he said.

I laughed. "Ooooooookay," I said. I was *pretty* sure he was just using it as a line—like he knew that saying he was a Breathalyzer salesman would appeal to a New Yorker who trafficked in irony, something I could tell my friends the next day over all-you-can-drink brunch while we snort-laughed our mimosas out of our noses, if I had been the type of New Yorker who went to all-you-can-drink brunches. I hadn't ever pictured what a Breathalyzer salesman looked like, but I would have put money on one being older, perhaps slightly heavyset.

Definitely wearing khakis. In fact, I hadn't ever considered where police departments procured Breathalyzers in the first place. Amazon? Breathalyzer dot-com? Definitely not from a twentysomething in Red Wing boots and a beanie visiting his friend in New York and going to an indie rock show.

We had sex—my first true one-night stand—and in the morning, as we were lying in bed, I said, "That was funny how last night you said you were a Breathalyzer salesman."

He laughed. "I *am* a Breathalyzer salesman."

"So wait," I said. "Really?"

"Really," he said. "I drive around and sell Breathalyzers to police departments." He paused and looked around my bedroom. "Can I ask how old you are?"

"I'm thirty," I said quickly. I was actually thirty-three, but I instinctively felt like I needed to take three years off my age. Why was he even asking, anyway? Wasn't asking someone's age one of those things you weren't supposed to do, especially after a one-night stand?

He seemed surprised. "Really? You're *thirty*?" He paused. "I wouldn't have guessed."

I laughed, a little nervously. Did he mean I didn't *look* thirty, or did he mean that he couldn't believe that a thirty-year-old was acting the way I was, getting drunk and taking a virtual stranger home and sleeping with him? But . . . didn't thirty-year-olds do that all the time? Even . . . thirty-three-year-olds? "How old are *you*?" I asked.

"Twenty-eight," he said. "I guess I was surprised that you're thirty because I'm the only one of my friends back home who still isn't married. So I was wondering if you were my age yet, but also, I guess I should have figured you were older because you live alone in New York."

"Oh, well, thanks," I said. "What's it like being the only single friend? I guess that's one good thing about living in New York—there are still plenty of single thirty-year-olds."

"Well, I live alone, but I own my house," he said.

"Wow," I said again, looking around the apartment that I shared only with my dog, Lee. I couldn't imagine being the only one of my friends who wasn't married at twenty-eight. Twenty-eight! I hadn't even met Jon, the first person I thought I *might* marry, at twenty-eight. Twenty-eight was when I had gone back to school, when I had left Philly for good, when I shared a shitty apartment with Alison on a shitty block in Williamsburg. My life had barely begun at twenty-eight.

After he left, I noticed the Revenge Jacket on the floor; I must have just tossed it when we had come in the night before. I sat down on my couch and held it for a moment. Where did Revenge Jacket Doree end and where did the "real" me begin? It was getting exhausting, feeling like I was toggling between identities. How much more validation from men would be enough?

A COUPLE OF WEEKS later, I was once again at the bar down the street, the one where I'd met Tim—who thankfully wasn't working that night—for a friend's birthday party. There was a guy there, Louis, who had been a couple of years ahead of me in college. We weren't close friends, but we'd run in the same social circles. I hadn't seen him much since college, but he looked the same, like a perpetual grad student, but an incredibly hot perpetual grad student. He was soft-spoken, with delicate tortoiseshell glasses, and a wry affect. In college, Daniel and I had both crushed on him from afar, in the way that you might admire a famous person, always referring to him by his full name: Louis Foster.

"Doree!" he said. Louis seemed genuinely pleased to see me. "How *are* you?" We started talking, and as the night wore on, we retreated to a nook by the window, and then we looked up and we were the only ones left from the party.

"So . . . do you live around here?" he asked. I nodded. "Do you want to get out of here?"

I did. I felt like this was the culmination of my ugly-duckling-turning-into-a-swan moment—*I was going to hook up with Louis Foster. This was really happening.* I thought back to college, when I was a sophomore and he was a senior, and whenever I'd see him at a party, usually with his messenger bag and wool crewneck sweater, I would literally swoon. I resisted the urge to text Daniel, to give him an update in real time. He was going to *die* when I told him.

We got back to my place and immediately made our way to the bedroom, and very quickly, before I really knew what was happening, we were naked. "Um," I said, hesitating, "I don't want to have sex." It would have been so easy to just have sex with Louis, but something was holding me back. It was almost as if now, ten years after college, I still couldn't totally believe it was happening, and if I slept with him, then my crush-from-afar would turn into an obsession.

He scoffed. "What, are you afraid I'm not going to be *nice* to you if we have sex?" He practically spat it out.

I was so taken aback, I didn't know how to respond. So *this* was who he was? "I . . . don't know," I said, faltering. The air in the room changed, and suddenly I didn't even want to make out with him anymore. "But I just don't." He seemed put out,

like he had had a very specific vision of how the night was
going to go, and then it didn't go that way, and he was going
to make sure I knew it. He didn't press it, though, and we
eventually fell asleep. In the morning, it seemed like he'd forgotten the conversation. We made out a little bit more, and as
he left, he said he'd call me.

He didn't call me the next day, or the day after, and after a
week I realized he was never going to call, and then I felt pathetic that even after he had been so mean I still wanted him
to call. I no longer felt like a swan; I felt like an ugly duckling
who had grown up into a marginally more attractive duck, like
a duck who had gotten her braces off but would always be a
duck. And ducks are cute, but they're not swans.

"I can't believe you hooked up with Louis Foster, oh my
god," Daniel said when I told him that Louis and I had gone
home together. "So what was he *like?*"

"Honestly?" I said. "He was kind of an asshole."

A FEW DAYS LATER, I got an email from Karen's boyfriend, who
lived with her in Washington, D.C., asking if he could call me
the next day to discuss something. "Of course," I responded.

"Hey, so, I've decided to propose to your sister," he said
when we got on the phone. I had just left the gym and was
walking down the street in the West Village. I stopped in a
doorway. "And I wanted to let you know."

"Congratulations!" I said. "That's so exciting. When are
you going to do it?"

I was happy for her, but it also just cemented for me how
upside down I felt about my place in my family. My sister was

twenty-six, a full seven years younger than me, and she was already getting engaged. Meanwhile, I was sleeping with Breathalyzer salesmen, not sleeping with college crushes, and inventing elaborate fantasies centered around a leather jacket. It was clear which one of us had grown up first. How much longer could I tell myself I was just taking time to figure things out?

CHAPTER SEVEN

My love life wasn't the only aspect of my life that felt like it was in purgatory. I was also spinning my wheels work-wise; freelancing was a grind, with no real end in sight. I'd taken a part-time job working at the *New York Daily News,* one of the city's tabloid newspapers, to make sure I could pay my rent. As I biked up the Hudson River Greenway to the paper's office on a warm September morning, I felt myself starting to sweat—first just a trickle down my face, then under my arms and in my crotch. *"Crap,"* I thought as I passed the Chelsea Piers complex in the west twenties. I still had ten more blocks to go before I would peel off at West Thirty-third Street and ride half a block up to the *Daily News* building, and I'd have to quickly wipe myself down before I went inside.

The building was a drab, hulking, sand-colored brutalist pyramid on possibly the least attractive block in all Manhattan, adjacent to a parking lot and across from a weedy vacant lot and busy Lincoln Tunnel ramp. The lobby was dark and run-down; everyone who went in and out looked like they would rather be literally anywhere else. The *Daily News* office itself wasn't much better—it was brighter, but only because of the harsh fluorescent lights; the carpet was worn; it had a general air of melancholy. The men wore khakis and the women all had office cardigans. I was working for the features editor, a skinny Irish woman named Dearbhla with dyed blond hair. She was a classic tabloid editor in the UK mold. She smoked cigarettes in her office, barely ate, and seemed to drink a lot. She had reporters who were her favorites and others who seemed to always be on her shit list. Dearbhla put entire emails into subject lines, as though she was so busy that she couldn't be bothered to click through to the "compose" box ("Any chance you know where the booze cake book is? Txs D"). But because I was part-time, floating in and out of the office, she treated me kindly, and it was steady, if not particularly stimulating, work. I needed the money, since my only other source of income was freelance writing, which was a constant hustle that paid inconsistently.

That day, as soon as I got upstairs to the features floor, I headed straight to the bathroom to wipe myself off and apply some makeup. It was one of those bathrooms with a distinct public bathroom smell, single-ply toilet paper, and rough paper towels dispensed from a metal dispenser. I dabbed concealer under my eyes, but it didn't stay because I was still too sweaty. I stared at my reflection and sighed. *Get me out of here,* I thought. I needed a job—a real job, one that didn't depress me every time I walked into the office, where I could feel like I was actually working toward something that mattered.

A few weeks later, I saw a job posting on the industry job board Mediabistro for a senior editor for *Rolling Stone*'s website. I wouldn't have described myself as a music editor, but I'd written about music, and, I realized, I sort of knew the editor in chief of the website from Twitter. I sent him a direct message saying that I was considering applying for the job, and did he have any thoughts or advice?

After I sent in my résumé, he asked me to come in for an interview. The magazine was in one of those Midtown buildings that I pictured when I thought about Powerful New York Media, like the Time-Life Building or the Seagram Building. It was a block from Radio City Music Hall, and the magazine's office was on the second floor, so the editors all had offices with big windows directly overlooking Fifty-second Street. It felt fancy—a far cry from a SoHo storefront or a drab building next to the West Side Highway—and I found myself drawn in by this fanciness. There was a hallway of every *Rolling Stone* cover ever published, and original artwork everywhere. *Rolling Stone* had started in the late sixties by tweaking the establishment, and now they *were* the establishment. They had grown up. Maybe it was time for me to do that, too. A few days later they offered me the job. It felt like things were finally getting back on track.

One night, not long after I was offered the *Rolling Stone* job, I came home and when my dog, Lee, came to greet me, her back half buckled and collapsed. I didn't know what to do, so I called Jon. I'd run into him a few weeks earlier and promised to let him see Lee if I thought she was getting close to the end, and this seemed like if it wasn't the end, then it was at the very least not good. I got his voicemail. I called Emily, my former Gawker co-worker who'd become a close friend. She came over, and then Jon called back, and then the three of us were in my apartment with Lee, waiting for a pet ambulance to take us to the twenty-four-hour emergency hospital.

I picked her up a couple of days later. She had had a stroke, the vet told me, and showed me some exercises I could do with

Lee's hind legs. The vet said if Lee was going to get better, she'd show progress soon. In the meantime, at home, I tried to make her as comfortable and happy as possible. She was still eating and seemed in good spirits; I gave her lots of salami; we sat on the couch and I rubbed her muzzle. She was going to be okay, I told myself. *We* were going to be okay.

EVERY MORNING AT *Rolling Stone,* there was a meeting with the magazine's editors, where we discussed what was going on in the music world and what we should be covering. My job was to assign and edit posts about the day's music news, but after I'd been there a few days, I realized that there were only a few staff writers, mostly the younger ones, who would agree to write anything for the website. The editors and the more experienced staff writers would say, "Oh, that's good for the web," but not volunteer to write it themselves. There was also a shared vocabulary among the mostly male staff that I was frantically trying to become familiar with. They'd say things like, "Marilyn's supposed to be getting us the new album tomorrow" and everyone would nod sagely, as I racked my brain to try to remember which musician Marilyn was a publicist for.

The hierarchy at the magazine was clear: On top were the people who worked on the print magazine (again, almost all men), who went to lunch together, gathered in the managing editor's office to loudly debate things like who *really* was the best guitarist of all time, and were asked to listening sessions where publicists would come to the office to play advance copies of sought-after albums. Those who had been invited would gather in the managing editor's office—ten feet from my desk—to listen on his state-of-the-art sound system, blasting

the music and talking loudly enough that it was hard to con-
centrate.

I went back and forth with myself about whether these
were deliberate snubs, or if it just literally did not occur to
them to invite me, and then I debated with myself about
which was worse. Better to be thought of and dismissed, or
not thought of at all?

Whether deliberate or not, it was clear that those of us who
worked for the magazine's website were at the bottom of the
hierarchy, the junior varsity squad. We were allowed to come
to the morning meetings, but we were excluded from pretty
much everything else. This was a common arrangement at
print magazines and newspapers. The print publications were
considered prestigious, their writers and editors paid better,
and the websites were for their scraps. Big stories would be
"saved" for the print edition, and there was barely any recognition if something resonated online. I'd experienced some of
this when I worked at the *Observer* and my story about the
so-called Hipster Grifter—who had scammed boyfriends and
roommates out of money, faked pregnancies and cancer diagnoses, and hustled her way into a job at *Vice* while being
wanted in Utah on fraud charges—had gone viral, and the top
editors at the paper had barely noticed, even though the story
was the most popular one to ever run on the website. Most
print editors and writers saw it as an insult if their story got cut
from the print edition and only ran online, but they all assumed
that their stories *would* go viral when they did get posted online. There was no understanding of what it took to write a
good story for the web, or that it actually took skill to write a
story online that people wanted to read. To me, it was bonkers
that you could write a story and not know exactly how many

people had read it. I loved the feedback loop of online writing; I thought most print-only writers were dinosaurs who also acted as gatekeepers. The web was a much more democratic place, and they didn't like that.

My boss—the one I'd reached out to on Twitter—was a skinny guy named Alec who vaguely, if you squinted, resembled a young Al Pacino. Alec was not around very much, I started to notice. One morning around eleven, I was at my desk, working on the day's stories; Alec, who sat in the cubicle next to me, was absent, and I hadn't heard from him regarding his whereabouts. Suddenly, the magazine's executive editor was standing in front of Alec's cubicle, looking extremely annoyed.

"Do you know where Alec is?" he asked me.

"I don't," I said. "Sorry."

"Our story's not on the website!" he said. I was silent. It was Alec's job to get the print stories up on the website, not mine. He stood there for a moment, as though waiting for me to come up with a solution. Finally, he said, "Just tell him to come see me when he gets in, okay?"

"Yup," I said. The executive editor wasn't technically my boss, but I knew he could make things uncomfortable for me if he wanted to. I hated this feeling, of sort of having to cover for Alec, but also that this was somehow my fault that the story wasn't on the website, or that I had the authority to fix it. It seemed like a classic trap that women in the workplace find themselves in: We are put in positions without any real power, and yet we are expected to clean up the messes of those who are.

CHAPTER EIGHT

One night a couple of weeks after I'd started the new job, I got home and Lee had pooped in her bed in the living room and hadn't touched her food. After her stroke, it had been getting increasingly difficult to get her to go outside. I called her vet and told her what was going on.

"The humane thing to do, at this point, is to end her misery," she said. "We can do it tomorrow, if you want."

Jon came with me to euthanize her. We sat with her on the floor as the vet inserted the medication that would kill her. It was quick, and she didn't seem to be in pain. Tears streamed down my face as Jon and I hugged goodbye. Lee had been my last real connection to him, and now that chapter of my life was truly over.

I got on the subway and went to my gym. I needed a distraction; I couldn't go home. I put on my bathing suit and got in the pool. The water was chilly, and even though I had stopped crying, I was having trouble getting my goggles to stick to my face. But then I put out one arm, then the other, and swam and swam and swam for what felt like hours.

When I got home, I opened the door and Lee's absence hit

me. I took her collar and leash out of my bag and hung it on a hook in the closet and tried not to cry again. The apartment felt depressingly empty. I kept replaying the last night of Lee's life in my mind—how she had dragged herself into my bedroom and slept by my bed, which she had never done, and how I had cried myself to sleep. I tried not to seem too melancholy at work, but one morning, a few days after Lee had died, I looked up at work and someone was standing at my cubicle. It was my co-worker Andrew.

"I'm really sorry about your dog," he said gently. "If you ever want to just like, hang out with another dog, you can come hang out with my dog."

"I don't think I'm ready for that, but thanks," I said. Andrew was cute, I thought. He looked vaguely Aryan—pale and blond, with small blue eyes. He wore plaid shirts and dark jeans, like pretty much every other guy on staff, and had a softly wry voice.

"You know, I've read your work," he said. "I was excited when I heard you were coming to the magazine."

I was flattered. Maybe there was actually one person here who didn't care that I didn't know the track listings for every single one of Bruce Springsteen's albums. "That's really nice, thanks," I said.

Soon, he came by my desk again. "I thought you'd like this," he said. It was a new book on the history of the business of hip-hop.

"Thanks," I said. It did look interesting, but even more than that, it felt like it was possible that Andrew really got me, or at least bothered to see me as someone who wasn't just a website drone. Andrew started following me on Twitter, then sent me a friend request on Facebook. A few days later, he forwarded me an email to my personal email address from a Park Slope dog rescue for a dog that needed a foster home. "Just in case you felt like a few days of canine company," he wrote. Soon, we were gossiping about co-workers and sharing jokes. He started asking me if I wanted anything every time he went to the little coffee shop across the street. He sent me a download of the Mountain Goats album *Tallahassee*, just because he thought I needed to own it, and if I already did own it, he asked why I hadn't yet brought it up in conversation. (I already owned it.) He was flirting, and I was more than happy to flirt back.

He seemed like an appropriate workplace crush. But then someone casually mentioned Andrew's girlfriend, one of the magazine's fact-checkers. *Girlfriend?* He had very much not mentioned a girlfriend, let alone one who worked with us. Then I realized who she was, a quiet blonde named Lauren who looked like she and Andrew were distantly related. I didn't trust people who went out of their way not to mention their significant others. It's not that hard to just casually slip a mention into conversation, like, "Oh, my girlfriend—have you met her yet? She's a fact-checker—really likes that album." Just, you know, as an example.

But he hadn't done that, and now I was blindsided. *I should probably not have a crush on someone with a girlfriend,* I thought, although it was really just a harmless little work crush, so what did it matter? And it was a distraction from the loneliness I was feeling—with Lee gone, the solitude of my new life was really sinking in. But even though I kept trying to tell myself it was just a work crush, Andrew continued to bring me coffee. He walked me to the train after work; he and Lauren never seemed to be leaving at the same time, but we, somehow, did.

Then he asked if I wanted to get drinks some night after work. *It's just a work crush,* I said to myself, as I emailed him back: "Sure!" *Keep things light and casual.*

"Lauren and I are having some trouble," he finally told me. "We're probably going to break up." His brow was furrowed, his voice breaking a little.

"I'm so sorry," I said. He was confiding in me, I thought— surely, this was a good thing? I didn't think about or talk to Lauren. I didn't *want* to know her side of the story; if Andrew said they were having issues, then she must have felt the same way. Maybe Lauren herself was instigating their issues and wanted to break up! Andrew *did* seem really upset about it, after all.

One evening after work, we shared a train ride back to his neighborhood and took a walk with his dog. Lauren wasn't home. Andrew seemed skittish, like he didn't want to be seen with me. I wasn't sure if he was nervous about running into Lauren, or if somehow seeing me on his home turf was disori- enting. Maybe whatever fantasy he'd had about me wasn't holding up. I wasn't sure how to feel—perhaps it was better if I just backed away slowly from the situation and pretended it never happened. But I couldn't. I now had a hardcore, couldn't- shake-it crush. I obsessed over Andrew's every move at work, dissected his emails to me, wondered what he was doing at night. Was he thinking about me as much as I was thinking about him?

A few days later, Andrew emailed me that he and Lauren had broken up and he was leaving their apartment that night. "I feel like absolute hell. I'm not sure I can really go through with this," he wrote. "Thanks again for hanging out. I'll do my best to not make this situation any weirder than it already is."

I read this email over several times. By "go through with this," did he mean "break up with Lauren"? Why did he seem so conflicted about someone he said he wanted to break up with so badly?

I wondered what this email was supposed to mean. He still brought me coffee and sent me flirty emails, but it seemed like the situation was weighing on him, which he kept me abreast of in great detail. I felt like maybe I shouldn't know these details about his relationship, but I also wanted them; they confirmed that they weren't right for each other—right?

This went on for a few more weeks, until it was time for the *Rolling Stone* holiday party, which was going to be held at a bar in the East Village. "I'm not going to go," he told me, as I stood by his cubicle. "I'm worried . . ." He paused and looked around, as though someone might be listening. "I'm worried Lauren is going to be . . . *violent.*"

A few minutes later, I got an email from him. "Lauren knows we've been talking," he wrote to me. "She's extremely pissed—at me, not you. I'm really sorry for dragging you into this."

I forwarded his email to Alison. "Can you believe this shit?" I wrote. For a while now, Alison had been not so subtly encouraging me to step away from the situation, pushing the theory that Andrew and Lauren had enlisted me as a sort of pawn in a revenge game they had going. She wrote back: "They were obviously bored with their lives, and now they're really enjoying this bit of drama." It had taken me months, but finally the endless back-and-forth, the secrets—it was obvious, in a way it hadn't been before, that Andrew was telling Lauren one thing and telling me another. I felt stupid for falling for it.

He had made it clear that ultimately whatever he felt for

me was eclipsed either by what he felt for Lauren or the drama that my having a crush on him had created in their relationship, and I needed to move on. I thought about that old chestnut of "when people tell you who they are, believe them." Andrew was telling me exactly who he was in seven-foot-tall neon signage. What had I been *thinking*? I resolved to ignore him, to decline his offers of coffee, and try to move on.

It worked for a couple of weeks. I was able to put him out of my mind, even though I had to see him every day. But soon, he started sending me emails and advance copies of albums again. He brought me coffee when I didn't ask for it. He told me he missed me. Finally, he said that Lauren had officially moved out and asked if we could maybe hang out again sometime.

This is a terrible idea, I thought . . . and agreed to do it anyway. I was still attracted to him, even after everything that had happened. I was also curious—what if it turned out that we had an amazing sexual connection and were destined to be together? Maybe the story of how we met would become a funny cocktail party anecdote—"Can you believe Andrew was actually dating someone else *in our office* when we met?!" Har, har, har, pass the truffled almonds! Plus, I had *won*. Lauren had moved out! He had chosen *me*.

I went over to his apartment. It looked like half his furniture was gone. We had sex that was reminiscent of an oil derrick drilling into the ground, where I was the ground and his dick—which was kind of grossly meaty—was the derrick. There had been almost no foreplay, just his pale body suddenly naked and on top of me. I stared up at the ceiling and thought, *This is what Lauren was fighting for?* It was the kind of sex where you're embarrassed for the person you just had it with because *they* clearly thought it was good sex, and you don't want to have to be the one to tell them that actually, just because you have a big dick does not mean you are good at sex, and in fact perhaps having a big dick makes it even more likely that you will be *bad* at sex, because you take it for granted that you will be good at it. I couldn't even muster up the energy to fake an orgasm.

In the morning, I woke up early and wondered what the protocol was. Should I sneak out? Were we going to have breakfast together? "Hey," he said, waking up. "I was thinking I'd make a pork roast today. Do you want some?"

"Um, sure," I said.

"It reminds me of being back home in Michigan," he said. "It's also one of the only dishes I know how to cook."

The recipe turned out to be a pork roast with a can of Campbell's Cream of Mushroom soup poured over it and baked. "So I know all her stuff is gone, but Lauren still has a key to the apartment," he said as we ate the pork roast.

"Wait, *what?*" I said.

"Yeah," he said. "So I guess she could probably walk in at any moment."

"So you're telling me she also could have walked in at any moment last night," I said. I couldn't believe he hadn't told me this. I felt violated, like I had once again been outwitted by him and Lauren. *He probably* told *her that I was coming over,* I thought suddenly, and felt sickened.

"I should go," I said, taking the plate to the sink. "I'll see you at work?"

Monday came, and it was time to go back to the office. Along with the regular spate of emails from publicists pitching their bands' news, Andrew continued to email me. He sent me pictures of his dog and links to videos he thought I'd find funny, but also emails about how he felt so terrible about how he was hurting Lauren, but that it also wasn't fair to me. And could we talk? Or no, actually, let's not talk, I can't talk to you, it's too painful. Wait, I've changed my mind. Let's talk.

The sad thing was that I was still attracted to him, even after all the mind games and the bad sex, and a part of me still held out hope that somehow things would magically work out between us. It didn't help that at the same time he was telling me that he needed to tend to Lauren's feelings, it felt like he had studied a manual of me and managed to pinpoint exactly what would lure me back in—he was giving me *just* enough to keep me interested, and then pulling back as soon as it seemed like I reciprocated his feelings. But even as I recognized his sociopathic manipulation, I couldn't bring myself to reject it. Lauren, meanwhile, sent me an email telling me that Andrew had been hooking up with random people he'd met on Craigslist and asked how that made me feel. I didn't respond.

I tried to extract myself from the situation, but it wasn't easy. He just wouldn't leave me alone, even as he told me how he wanted to leave me alone, and I was having a lot of trouble trying to move on, because he sat ten yards away from me and I saw him every day.

Finally, I told him it would be better if we stopped talking. "It's for the best," Meera reassured me, when I told her things were over. She was kind and supportive, but I knew she and the rest of my friends had grown tired of the drama of their thirty-three-year-old friend acting like a high school sophomore who got all her relationship tips from *Seventeen* magazine.

In April, I was in my apartment with some friends, having

a casual Passover seder, when I saw an email from Andrew come in on my phone. We hadn't spoken much in the last few weeks, and I had started casually seeing someone else, a guy I'd met at South by Southwest named Dustin who was Andrew's polar opposite—an evangelical Christian who worked in tech and was earnestly enthusiastic about everything; he was like an excitable Labrador puppy—and I had started to feel that I was finally, maybe, truly over Andrew. I went into the kitchen to read it by myself. It said: "Hey. So Lauren and I are kind of seeing each other again. I'm not sure it's the most brilliant idea; it just kind of happened. I'm also not sure I need to be telling you this, but I figure the best thing to do is say something before you saw us together or something. If I'm wrong about that, I'm sorry. I'm still sad circumstances weren't right for you and me. I really hope you're doing well."

"Everything okay?" Dustin asked when I rejoined him and the rest of my friends in the living room.

"Oh yeah," I said. "Actually, everything is *great*."

CHAPTER NINE

Even though the situation with Andrew was finally, truly over, and Dustin was a welcome distraction, I couldn't stop thinking about what a melodramatic waste the past few months had been. Now that it was over, what had I learned? That I could be easily targeted by master manipulators? Or—and this was a scarier thought—maybe Andrew *wasn't even that great of a manipulator.* Maybe I was just an exceptionally easy mark for someone who knew to look for my particular combination of outward bravado and inward insecurity. Again, I felt like my desperate need for validation, especially when it came to my looks and attractiveness, had won out over rationality. I had thought Andrew could see the "real" me, but he had just been able to exploit my insecurities. It turned out that Revenge Jacket Doree was just the same old me in a slightly sexier getup. I had thought she represented moving forward, but maybe she was just holding me back.

Things petered out with Dustin when it became clear that he hadn't left his evangelicalism as far back in the past as he had made it seem—he asked me, with no trace of irony, whether I had ever considered becoming a Jew for Jesus, and when I tried to explain that Jews for Jesus are a fringe, cultlike group who are not actually Jews, he seemed let down, like he had figured out this loophole that would allow me to remain Jewish and him to not feel guilty about dating someone who wasn't saved. But I wasn't especially broken up about Dustin. There was someone else on the horizon. And he was someone I had never thought would actually be interested in me, mostly because he was legitimately *hot*.

Dustin was handsome, but Luke had the rugged kind of hotness that radiated that old saying, "Men want to be him and women want to be with him." He was tall and tan, with black hair that he wore up in a bun, and a wide, easy smile. (I previously would not have pegged myself as someone who would be attracted to a man bun, but it turns out that being incredibly hot means you can wear a man bun.) In my head, I had just been admiring him from afar, in the same way that Daniel and I had admired Louis Foster in college. But the fact is that Luke had slid into my Twitter DMs first—innocuously and casually, but *definitely* first. I had tweeted something about how Target had moved everything around and I couldn't find anything, and he messaged me that he had just been there, too, and it was overwhelming and he just needed a picture frame. But I didn't really think anything of it—he was friendly whenever he came by the office, so surely this was just Luke being friendly old Luke. Hot people *are* allowed to be friendly—right?

Oh yeah: Luke also worked for *Rolling Stone*. Which, given my track record, probably should have warned me off right away. But, I reasoned, he didn't work out of the office all the time—he was a contributing writer, so he popped up periodically when he was finishing up a piece or had a meeting with an editor. He'd initially come by my cubicle a few months earlier, when he was working on a story about a musician who was in prison, and asked if I had any tips for how to best ensure that he'd be able to talk to the musician when he got out. I was flattered. Luke was a darling of the magazine's editors; he got the plum assignments, and here he was, asking *me* for reporting advice. *Well then!* After the initial Twitter DM he sent me about Target, he popped up in my DMs periodically that spring, recommending barbecue places in Austin and offering to lend me *Friday Night Lights* DVDs.

His inconsistent office visits were how I justified developing just the *teensiest, tiniest* of crushes on him. Really, it wouldn't be like the Andrew situation, at all, I told myself—first, because there was no way in hell Luke would actually be interested in me, and, second, because he was rarely around. There was no chance of a bad, embarrassing breakup that everyone in the office knew about and where I'd have to see the person day after day after day. After day. And the day after that. And, third, it wasn't exactly a *crush;* I mean, I barely knew the guy. It was more of an *appreciation.* I could appreciate Luke's attractiveness in the same way I could appreciate that Brad Pitt is attractive! If that meant I was objectifying him, so be it. He also barely had any social media footprint, besides Twitter, which was both appealing and frustrating, because how was I supposed to stalk his social media if he barely had any social media?

It was fun to flirt with someone so hot, but it also felt safe. Again, there was *no way,* I told myself, that he would possibly be interested in me. After all, I am a person who has hated pretty much every photo ever taken of herself, except for a couple of selfies where the lighting was perfect and I was able to take approximately five hundred pictures before I found one that was acceptable to post on social media. Luke, on the other hand, had been "papped" while interviewing a very handsome famous actor, and the paparazzi just assumed he was one of the actor's friends, because he was just as hot as the actor was. Yes, I had a little crush on him, but his hotness was an objective *fact*. If someone took a candid photo of me walking down the street, I would undoubtedly be scowling, they would get my "bad" side, and I'd be wearing my most unflattering outfit, and it would be like one of those mean photos that the tabloids take when the headline reads, "Can You Believe What [Formerly Attractive Famous Actress] Looks Like Now?"

So that summer, when Luke resurfaced at the office, I was still content with swooning from a safe (physical, emotional) distance. But then he came by my desk and I blurted out that we should get barbecue sometime, since he seemed to know so much about it, being from Texas and all, and he said, "Oh, yeah, we should," but in a way where I was convinced he was just saying that to be nice, because hot people are nice to not-hot people so they don't feel bad, but to my surprise he followed up with an email. "We shouldn't lose momentum!" he wrote, and then a few days later we were on . . . a date? It wasn't clear to me, even when he paid for my dinner and we talked for so long that the barbecue place conspicuously started to close. He was funny, clearly very smart, and still blindingly hot. This was where being debilitatingly insecure came into play, because I still—*still!*—was not convinced that he like-liked me, as we used to say in seventh grade.

"We didn't make out or anything," I told Alison the next day. "So—I don't know? It was *maybe* a date? I think I might like him. This was just supposed to be a crush. Oh god."

"It was a date," she said firmly. "It was a *date*! You went on a date with Luke."

"Well . . . he did email me to say he had a great time," I said. "I guess that's something you say to someone you just went on a date with, right?"

We emailed back and forth for a couple of days—I tried to keep the tone light and a little coy, even though what I really wanted to write was *DO YOU LIKE ME? BECAUSE I THINK THE TINY CRUSH I HAD ON YOU IS NOW A REAL CRUSH AND I CAN'T STOP THINKING ABOUT YOU AND DO YOU WANT TO HAVE SEX? AND ALSO, DO YOU LIKE ME?* Then he said he was leaving soon for Africa to play drums with a Britpop singer for a story, because that was the kind of life he led, but he suggested we hang out again when he got back into town. It took him a month to get back into town—a month where he sent me a few emails, each of which I immediately parsed for clues about his feelings for me—but when he did, we got dinner, and then drinks afterward, and then we made out in the doorway of a small bar in Carroll Gardens for half an hour. So I guess it was a date.

But then I didn't hear from him.

"So I guess we just made out, and now he's not interested," I said to Alison a few days later. Unfortunately for her, she was my premiere confidante for any and all Luke-related updates. "I mean, I haven't heard from him. I guess it's over."

The look she gave me said *you're being dramatic,* but she said, instead, "Are you *sure?* Didn't you say he was going somewhere?"

"Yeah," I said. "I think he's in Canada? Or Minnesota? I can't remember. He was going to one place, and then another place."

"He's probably really busy and doesn't have Wi-Fi," she said. "Did you email him?"

"No!" I said. "Of course not." I didn't want to seem desperate or needy, which was what I was convinced an email would telegraph to him.

"Maybe he doesn't think you're into him," she said.

This statement was so outrageous that I laughed. "I *doubt* it," I said.

He emailed a couple of days later as though I hadn't spent the last few days completely spiraling about every single comment I had made on our date, trying to figure out if *that* was the reason he had decided he didn't like me. But now, I realized, I had more than a crush. I had fallen for him, and hard. I told myself that Luke was everything I thought I wanted—superhot, supersmart, an amazing writer, and seemingly, if confusingly, into me—but even after just two dates, it was clear that any kind of relationship with him was going to be entirely on his terms: He was always out of town on assignment, and when he was in town, he was often on deadline for a story and could not be disturbed. There was something Easy Rider–ish about him; I could picture him on a motorcycle, man bun tucked beneath the helmet, driving off into the sunset, without out caring about anyone or anything. He also wrote for a men's magazine, and his assignments were a hilarious collection of men's magazine tropes: Drive, alone, across Alaska! Report on the nightlife scene in Johannesburg! Profile man's man Jon Hamm!

He eventually resurfaced. He'd been in Texas on assignment and wanted to know when we could hang out at my apartment and watch *Breaking Bad* together. I was thrilled, of course, and even more thrilled when he came over with a T-shirt he had brought me from his trip. So he *had* been thinking about me. But I was so nervous around him, and so convinced that if I said one wrong thing that he would just disappear forever, that I overcompensated by acting like I was *totally fine* with his schedule and his lack of communication and that my life was otherwise so thrilling that it really didn't bother me *at all;* I mean, for all he knew, maybe I wasn't even *that* attracted to him—right?

I had somehow internalized a combination of Carrie Bradshaw's toxic relationships; the *Sex and the City* mantra, later spun out into a book and a movie, of "he's just not that into you"; and the hipster version of the ideal woman, the Manic Pixie Dream Girl, who didn't even have to *think* about being cool, she just *was,* in part because she was so fucked-up that she needed men to "save" her. But I could out-cool anyone, I decided. So I waited to email or text him back, I didn't ask him to hang out, I never articulated to him directly how I felt. I had carefully cultivated a calm exterior, but inside, I was dying. Every time I saw his name pop up in my inbox it was like I had simultaneously hit a slot machine jackpot and I had also lost my last dollar at a slot machine. What if I opened it and he said he didn't want to see me anymore? But his emails were always long and detailed and just enough to reassure me that, *yes,* he was still interested in seeing me for no-strings-attached sex for the two days he was in town every month! And because, deep down, I still didn't think I deserved to be with him, I told myself that this was enough.

Whereas my situation with Andrew had been, embarrassingly, completely public knowledge at the magazine, my faux-lationship with Luke—as far as I knew—was not. And I intended to keep it that way—I didn't want to be known as the person who had hooked up with not just one, but *two* male staffers at the magazine in less than a year. The secrecy of the relationship made it exciting, but it also made it seem less real. When we were together, I could convince myself that everything about my relationship with him was great—I loved being with him, when I was with him. But as soon as he left, it was like he had never been there.

That said, when I really stopped to think about it, I honestly wasn't sure how I felt about him, beyond what still felt like a total infatuation. I didn't know him—not *really*. We'd been seeing each other for a couple of months but had only hung out a handful of times. I knew an *idea* of him that I had built up that was based partly on reality, but also on his emails, and also on what my fantasy of him looked like. I was able to project anything I wanted to onto him because he was so unavailable.

This continued for months. He would leave town, go silent on email, and then resurface once he was back in town and want to hang out. When we were actually together, it was great. He felt like my boyfriend. He came to my annual Hanukkah party, helped me clean up afterward, and then we had sex and snuggled all night. But trying to make concrete plans with him drove me crazy. I asked what he was doing for New Year's, and he said he wasn't sure, and I asked if he wanted to hang out; a friend, Nora, was having a low-key party. "Sure!" he wrote.

"Great!" I responded. "Maybe we can meet up before and grab dinner or something?"

And then he just . . . didn't respond. I was on a yoga retreat in Upstate New York with my friend Tess in the days leading up to New Year's, where we were supposed to be relaxing and reflecting on the year that was ending and setting intentions for the new year, and also eating a lot of very bland vegan food. In between yoga classes and meditation sessions I kept checking my phone—Had he texted? Emailed? He had not. (So much for practicing mindfulness.)

"I guess he's flaking on me," I said to Tess the night before we were going home.

"I'm sorry," she said. "Why don't you and I hang out, we can get dinner before Nora's party, and then if he surfaces he can come along?"

"That sounds great," I said, trying not to cry—both at his flakiness, and her kindness and willingness to be a third wheel.

The next morning, he texted. "Hey! Yes, sounds great," he wrote, as though I hadn't been waiting for his response for the last three days. He came out to dinner with Tess and me, then we met up with some other friends, one of whom had a car, so we drove to Nora's party in Prospect Heights. It felt like we were *together*. But it also felt fleeting, like the next morning he would go home and then I might not hear from him for weeks—which was, in fact, what happened.

He was infuriatingly aloof, and yet when he'd beckon, I'd always answer. Because I liked him, and because there was still a part of me that couldn't quite believe that I was with this guy.

I was convinced he was completely out of my league, looks-wise, and I'd never felt that way before about anyone I dated. Maybe it was good for me, I thought, to be seeing someone who was incredibly attractive? But instead of making me feel better about myself, it made me feel worse.

CHAPTER TEN

It never occurred to me to invite Luke to my sister's wedding. Even if we'd been seeing each other on a normal relationship cadence, we'd only been hanging out for three months or so—not long enough where I was ready to introduce him to my family, let alone ask him to be my date to a family wedding. But as I took the train to D.C. that Friday morning in November 2011, I couldn't help but think about the fact that I was going to my little sister's wedding alone. I was thirty-four, she was twenty-seven—shouldn't it have been the other way around?

I was excited for Karen, and excited to spend the weekend celebrating, but I also felt melancholy. When was it going to happen for me? Then I immediately felt guilty for feeling melancholy. This weekend shouldn't be about me, but it was hard not to feel constantly reminded that I was single and "old." At Karen's bachelorette party in August, I spent the weekend with her best friends from high school and college and sleepaway camp, all of whom were her age and half of whom were also either already married or engaged, and sporting large, shiny diamonds. They had law degrees and MBAs and beautifully blown-out hair. *They are on a different path,* I had to remind myself, but why wasn't I content to take that path, too? We played games, like one where Karen had to answer questions about her fiancé, Steve; someone had hired a stripper, who showed up in a cop's uniform. I'd never been to a bachelorette party before—my friends who were married either hadn't had them, or I wasn't close enough to them to have been invited.

At my sister's bridal shower, which I cohosted with my brother's fiancée (my brother and his fiancée had gotten engaged over the summer, so now I would *definitely* be the last of my siblings to get married, if I ever did) at her apartment on the Upper East Side, Karen's best friend sat next to her as she opened her presents, weaving the ribbons from the gift wrap into a hat. Where had she learned about this ribbon hat making? I wondered. I had never been to a bridal shower and I marveled at yet another "womanly" ritual that I had somehow completely missed. As we were about halfway through the gift opening, my mother whispered, "Where's your gift?"

"What do you mean?" I said. "I'm hosting the party. I didn't get her a gift."

My mother looked horrified. "You're *still supposed to get a gift!*" she said. "I can't *believe* you didn't get a gift."

"How was I supposed to *know*?" I said. I legitimately meant it. Suddenly, I was back at sleepaway camp, watching as Rachel applied lip gloss in the mirror so she could go meet her boyfriend in the soccer field, as Lisa shaved her legs in the middle of the girls' area the summer we were twelve, as the other girls wrote their letters home in bubble letters, putting hearts where the dot in the *i* went. Once again, it was as if when every other girl was born, a nurse had handed their parents a handbook with instructions on how to be a girl, but the day I was born, the copy machine at the hospital was broken and the nurse had just looked at me and told my parents, *Well, she'll just have to figure it out. I'm sure she'll be fine.*

And it *was* mostly fine, and I *had* figured out a lot of things for myself, and in fact, I had made the conscious choice to *not* participate in a lot of the things in the handbook, but every so often, I was reminded that this whole world of social codes and cues and expectations existed and I had just somehow . . . missed it? My sister hadn't missed it; my mom didn't seem to have missed it. But here I was, getting shamed for not bringing a gift to a bridal shower and watching as my sister put a hat made of ribbons on her head as everyone clapped. My sister and I were close—we texted and chatted on Gchat every day— but I'd never felt more like the moody Daria to her sunny, carefree Quinn.

In D.C., the day after I arrived, the other bridesmaids and I gathered in Karen's hotel suite to get ready. She had gotten all of us satin robes with our initials on them as bridesmaids' gifts. I also had never been a bridesmaid, and now, in my sister's hotel suite, as a hairstylist curled my hair and a makeup artist applied false lashes to my eyes, I made a mental note: If I ever got married, I should get my bridesmaids gifts.

All the bridesmaids had dresses in the same shade of purple silk. Most of my sister's friends were tiny; they looked like delicate violets, and I looked like Barney, towering over them in my uncomfortable heels. At the reception, I mostly stuck with my brother and his fiancée. My sister was drunk and happy, and I was happy for her. But for me, getting married had never seemed so far out of reach.

CHAPTER ELEVEN

A month later, a writer I knew mostly from the internet who'd worked at a bunch of the same places as me, but at different times, DMed me on Twitter. "Hey—want to get a cup of coffee sometime soon? I'm hiring cat picture aggregators and think you're a natural." It was Ben Smith, who had just been hired to take over editorial operations at BuzzFeed and start producing news. We had coffee, then a few days later met for beers in my neighborhood, and he told me about his vision for BuzzFeed, which was then known mostly as an aggregator and creator of viral internet content. Did I want to be a part of it, maybe overseeing entertainment, culture, and lifestyle?

I'd been at *Rolling Stone* for less than a year and a half, but even setting aside the Andrew debacle, it had become increasingly clear that it wasn't a good fit. I just could not get excited about another Black Keys magazine cover, and editing daily music news stories was starting to feel like an unrewarding grind. My boss, Alec, had finally gotten fired over the summer, but the replacement they'd brought in was a guy from AOL with a mandate for one thing and one thing only: increase website traffic. The way to do this, he decided, was to just publish a *lot*. The newsworthiness and quality didn't necessarily matter; what mattered was that there were new items up on the site all the time. The problem was that there often just wasn't enough interesting music news in a day, so the definition of what qualified as "news" got stretched and stretched, with stories like "Whitney Houston Nearly Kicked Off Flight" and "Nickelback Respond to Haters on Twitter."

The difference between the magazine and the website had never felt starker. Jann Wenner, the *Rolling Stone* founder who remained in charge (even if he wasn't in the office five months out of the year, jetting off to one of his several other homes around the world), still saw the magazine as his crown jewel. It felt like the website was almost dirty to him, just a way to make money and compete with the rest of the content mills.

I was hardly a content snob—we'd had post quotas at Gawker, and I was just as obsessed with web traffic as anyone else. But unlike anyone I'd ever worked for, my new boss seemed uniquely uninterested in what we were publishing. It *truly* did not seem to matter to him, as long as we were getting more traffic. There was something almost nihilistic about his disinterest. The people I used to work for at least *pretended* to care. *Rolling Stone* crystallized for me the idea that at the bare minimum, I needed to feel like my work mattered to someone. Otherwise, what was the point? I had taken the job because I thought it would give me more pride in my work than freelancing and working part-time at the *Daily News,* but it hadn't.

So Ben's offer intrigued me. I'd be able to hire people. I could publish stories that I thought mattered. I'd have influence. People would, theoretically, listen to me. Maybe this

would be the job that finally made me feel like I had a purpose. After a couple more meetings, BuzzFeed offered me a
job.

On my last day at *Rolling Stone,* an email popped up from
Andrew: "Good luck to you; I'm kind of jealous. Maybe we
can catch up someday." As far as I knew, he and Lauren still
lived together—and yet, he was still fishing to see if he could
get any reaction from me. *I'm done feeding your ego,* I thought
and didn't respond. Was this what they would call . . . growth?

A COUPLE OF WEEKS after I got the BuzzFeed job offer, Luke and
I got dinner in the West Village. I was excited to see him, but
nervous—a couple of days earlier, I'd finally sent him an email
that told him, more directly than I ever had before, that I
found his hot- and coldness hard to deal with, and it made me
question where things stood with him. He had responded only
to the part of the email about making plans, which made me
apprehensive—and a sign of my insecurity over the relationship that I didn't feel comfortable pushing him on it. But that
night, everything seemed fine. After dinner, we headed to the
IFC Center movie theater on Sixth Avenue to see *Pina,* the
Wim Wenders documentary about the choreographer Pina
Bausch. The movie was excellent, but I was distracted, worrying about where things stood between us. Then we headed
back to my apartment, and I brought up the email, and once
I started talking I couldn't stop. It was hard for me, I said, how
he just disappeared for days and sometimes weeks at a time.
Even if he was out of town, I needed *some* communication.
And what *was* our whole thing, anyway? We had never had the
"define the relationship" talk; I had once asked him if he was

sleeping with other people, and he had said no, but I wasn't sure if I totally believed him.

"We are going on occasional dates and having no-strings-attached sex when it is convenient for me—were you under the impression that this was anything else?" he said. Okay, fine, he didn't say this, but I kind of wish he had, because at least he would have been honest. But the thing I would later realize about guys like Luke is they also have a pathological aversion to anyone hating them. Luke's actual job was to pretend he liked the people he was interviewing, so that these people would trust him, like him, and then, in the cloud of that warmth and trust, say things they'd later end up regretting. So assuaging the truth was second nature to Luke. You'd never catch him in an actual *lie,* but you could also never be sure that what he was telling you was the whole truth. So what he *actually* said was "I feel terrible, I just don't think I can be that person. I wish you had said something earlier." He paused. "You know, I felt like you were never really 'in it.' Like, I didn't really know what was going on between us."

Oh. So it was *my* fault. I started to cry. The conversation confirmed everything I had been afraid of: I had been so worried about scaring him off by telling him how I really felt, that my playing it cool had backfired and now he just saw me as a casual hookup, nothing more. And maybe it *had* been my fault. Maybe if I hadn't been so determined to be the person I thought he wanted me to be, I could have just been myself—and maybe he would have liked that person even more than the person I was trying, and failing, to be.

"Will you . . . stay here tonight?" I asked. I felt humiliated, but I also didn't want to be alone. "No sex. We can just sleep."

He left in the morning. I still couldn't believe what had

happened. That couldn't be it, right? It was over, just like that? How was it possible that at this time just *yesterday* I had been looking forward to seeing him, excited about talking about my new job with him, hopeful that we would have a conversation about my email that concluded with him declaring his love for me. Obviously that had been a fantasy, and I felt stupid for thinking it could have been any other way.

I'd had abrupt breakups before—the optician I'd dated in Philly in my mid-twenties had broken up with me after watching the French New Wave movie *Breathless* on my couch. The movie ended, he announced that *Breathless* made him realize we needed to break up, and he got up and left. Another time, my stoner art-student boyfriend stayed at my apartment when I left to walk the dog after a fight, and when I came back he was gone, with just a note on my computer that he had left. In retrospect, though, I'd been able to see both those breakups coming, and I ultimately wasn't devastated by them. This one felt both inevitable and shocking.

I couldn't think about much of anything else for weeks. I went to yoga and cried during Savasana, the corpse pose at the end of class. I constantly replayed in my head all the interactions we'd had and second-guessed every single thing I'd ever said to him. It took every ounce of self-control I had not to email or text him constantly, but over the next few weeks, I did send him a couple of innocuous, friendly emails, just because I felt like I needed to see his name in my inbox. I missed him so much—the way I'd missed him when he was away was *nothing* compared to how much I missed him now that I knew even our tenuous, not-really-a-thing thing was really and truly over. And now he responded to my emails immediately—which only made me feel worse, because it was a reminder of how long he'd taken to respond when we were ostensibly "dating." Maybe, I realized miserably, he hadn't taken so long to respond not because he was trying to play hard to get, but because he was trying to craft a perfect email to me, because *he* cared what *I* thought of him. Now that we were broken up, he didn't. My only tiny consolation was that I was in no danger of running into him at work—if I was on a motorcycle in Mongolia, maybe. But *definitely* not at work.

CHAPTER TWELVE

Things ending with Luke sent me on another existential spiral. I would be thirty-five in a couple of months—the age that I used to think was *so* old! The age when I assumed I would have my proverbial shit together! The age when I would not still be pining over a guy who did not reciprocate my feelings and crying over him in yoga! Thirty-five was the age that I'd been dreading ever since I watched my first episode of *Sex and the City*—it was the Rubicon where, once crossed, women shriveled up and became crones living forgotten and alone; my former Gawker colleague Alex jokingly referred to people's thirty-fourth birthdays as "last call," but the joke hit a little too close to home.

Throughout this period, the only thing that was keeping me somewhat sane was running. I had started running a few months before Jon and I had broken up. It was grueling and hard. My lungs burned at every step, my legs ached. In high school, I played lacrosse for two seasons because some of my friends were playing and I had nothing better to do, but I couldn't run very fast or very far, so they made me the goalie.

Instead of a cute little plaid skirt and polo shirt, I wore a big, hulking, padded uniform that covered almost every inch of my body, and a helmet. I waddled out onto the field and took my place in the net, mostly just waiting around until one of the girls from the other team—inevitably blond, long-limbed, and fast as hell—came charging down the field, hurling a small rubber ball extremely close to my face.

For close to two decades, I had been content to be someone who was emphatically *not* a runner. I didn't understand runners, didn't get how they could literally just *put on a pair of sneakers* and dash out the door. In my mind, runners were focused, determined people. Running itself seemed like a pursuit that was almost the opposite of how I saw myself—as an impatient person who preferred instant gratification to long-term planning—and I think that's why I wanted to get good at it, as though to show myself that I was capable of something I was convinced I wasn't.

I started by running on the treadmill at the gym, and then I was running the length of Court Street from the Carroll Gardens apartment I shared with Jon, and then I was doing that faster. It still didn't feel *great,* but charting my progress was immensely satisfying, both in terms of the number of miles I was running and how quickly I could do them. I did my first race that spring, a 10K in Central Park, and felt a sense of achievement that I'd never really felt before. It seemed so straightforward: Set a goal, achieve said goal through hard work and focus and determination, and get a flimsy participation medal and a T-shirt with a corporate sponsor emblazoned on it.

It occurred to me that, other than graduating from college,

there hadn't been that many things in my life where I'd actually articulated a goal that I wanted to achieve and plotted
exactly how I was going to reach it. Maybe getting good at
running would be my way into becoming a more focused person, instead of just flitting from job to job, boyfriend to boyfriend, apartment to apartment.

Then I found out that if I ran a certain number of races in
a year, I could qualify for the New York Marathon the following year. It seemed like a reasonable, if intimidating, goal. At
least one weekend a month I would have a race, usually in
Central Park, and by the end of 2011, I had run all the races I
needed to qualify. In January 2012, I officially was entered in
that year's New York City Marathon. I went into deep training
mode; I was running a few times a week, with a long run on
the weekends. It was winter, so I would put on my cold weather
running gear: running tights, a long-sleeve shirt, a light jacket,
gloves, a hat or fuzzy headband that covered my ears. Still, on
those long run days, when I would usually take the subway
into Lower Manhattan and run on the path along the Hudson
River, the wind whipped off the water, chapping my face and
making tears run from my eyes. Even though I wasn't *crying*
crying, it still felt cathartic.

At least I wasn't sitting around my apartment by myself,
moping about Luke, I reasoned. But even thinking about not
thinking about him meant that, yes, I was still thinking about
him. Random times we'd hung out when I'd felt happy would
pop into my head, like the time we sat at a bar and drew a
flimsy map of the United States from memory and filled in all
the states together and I couldn't remember the direction that
the hypotenuse of the triangles that formed New Hampshire

and Vermont went in. I didn't think about the times I waited for him to email me back, or when he would flake on plans and tell me his phone died, or when it felt like I was begging him to hang out with me.

I was able to keep it together at work, but at night, I felt lonely and despondent. In my darkest moments, I wondered why I hadn't just stuck it out with Jon. It hadn't been perfect, but was it any worse than how I was feeling? We'd definitely be engaged by now, I thought, if not already married. Maybe we'd have bought that apartment we'd always been talking about! Maybe I'd even be *pregnant*. After we'd broken up, I had chased the high highs that I thought I'd been missing with him, and now I was experiencing the lowest lows. Running was only going to get me so far, literally and figuratively.

I was on dating apps, and going on dates here and there, but I still couldn't let go of my feelings for Luke. One weekend afternoon a couple of months after Luke and I had broken up, I met Meera for coffee. "Is it crazy to say that it feels like things with him might not be totally over?"

She looked at me, slightly alarmed. "What do you mean?" she said carefully.

"No, I mean, I know we broke up," I said. "I guess I just mean that, like, there's a part of me that just feels like we could get back together, like we still have more to do, or something."

"I think it's okay to let yourself feel those things," she said. "I just . . . I wouldn't fixate on it, you know?"

I nodded. I knew she was right. I needed to move on.

FINALLY, I REALIZED I needed therapy. My daily Gchat sessions with my friends about the state of my romantic life were wearing on them, and I was having trouble escaping the well of self-pity I found myself in. If I really thought about it, I'd been stuck in the same pattern for the better part of ten years—dating someone seriously for a while, and then after breaking up with them, getting into torturous situations with guys I was usually infatuated with and who didn't totally feel the same way about me, but who strung me along and gave me enough crumbs that it was difficult to extricate myself from their spell. Some of my friends had been there for the duration. It was time—for my sake, and for theirs—to figure this shit out.

My friend Mandy sent me the name of a woman her therapist liked to refer people to. Her name was Cynthia, which seemed like a perfect therapist name—it connoted a woman of a certain age, who would be wise and warm. Cynthia was, in fact, all those things. She looked to be in her late forties or early fifties, and had curly gray hair that she wore piled on her head, and no makeup except for lipstick. She wore lots of button-down shirts and boots. I liked her immediately.

"So tell me why you decided to come to therapy," she said. I was sitting on a leather couch facing big windows that overlooked a busy SoHo corner not far from the old Gawker office.

"I broke up with someone a couple of months ago, and we weren't even really in a *relationship*, like I'm not even really sure *what* we were, and we were only 'together'"—I put this word in air quotes—"for like, five months or something." I took a breath. "But . . . I feel sadder about it than I feel like I should. Like the proportion of my sadness over this relationship doesn't make sense, for how long we were 'together.'" Again, the air quotes.

She contemplated this. "Why do you think that is?" I knew the question was coming, and still, I struggled to answer it.

"I guess . . . I mean, I *really* liked him," I said.

"What did you like about him?" she asked.

This was a more difficult question. "He was really . . . hot," I said. The word *hot* strobed in the air—neon teen pink. "Um, but also, he was really interesting and smart and he . . . wrote me really good emails? When he would email me."

"What do you mean?" she asked.

"Well, he just wasn't around very much," I said. "He writes for the magazine where I used to work, and they're always sending him on assignments in random places with, like, a day's notice. So he'd just disappear for a few days, or weeks. And then when he was on deadline he'd disappear but then he'd resurface as though nothing had happened."

"That sounds really frustrating," she said. "And like it was hard for you to get to know him."

"I mean, yeah," I said.

"Why do you think you were attracted to someone who wasn't around very much?"

Yowch. Cynthia's questions were all the ones that I had avoided asking myself over the last few months, and now, sitting across from her in this blandly comfortable room, I had nowhere to hide from them.

"Um . . ." I stalled. "Well. If someone's not around very much, and it's hard to get to know them, I guess it's easy to, like, project anything you want onto them. I guess in my mind I turned him into the person I wanted him to be, not the person he actually is."

She nodded. "He didn't give you enough data." She paused. "The way you responded to that is completely normal, by the way. When we don't have enough data, we tend to fill in the gaps ourselves. And that means it's easy to create a kind of fantasy of a person."

"Right," I said, turning this idea around in my mind. I also realized I hadn't responded to the rest of her question. "Do you . . . do you think it's possible that I was attracted to him because I felt like I didn't deserve to be with someone who was going to give me all of himself?"

"That's certainly possible," she said. "Is that what you think?"

I thought about the ways that I had felt so desperate for any scraps of attention from Luke, the anxious feeling I'd have as I waited for his emails and texts, how I made excuses for him about why he wasn't my boyfriend, how I had always felt like I wasn't pretty enough to be with him, how my friends had tried to tell me that I deserved more but I didn't want to listen to them.

"Yes," I said. "You know . . . I think in some ways I feel stuck. Like, even though I have this new job, I'm wondering where *I* am in all this. Who's steering the ship, I guess. Like it sometimes feels like I'm just sort of careening from one thing to the next, whether it is a guy or a job or . . . anything, really."

"It's just about time for us to stop," she said gently, glancing at the clock facing her on the table next to me. "Do you want to set something up for next week?"

The rest of the day, I couldn't get my conversation with Cynthia out of my head. I needed to go for a run—I didn't feel stuck when I went running, even though it was still a struggle. I liked the solitude. Even in the noise and chaos of the city, I could let my mind wander, and each mile that my running app told me I'd logged gave me a little jolt of satisfaction. The next morning, as I jogged north through my Fort Greene neigh-borhood, then past the Brooklyn Navy Yard and up into Wil-liamsburg, the sweat dripped down my forehead but my lungs weren't burning, my legs weren't aching. I wasn't especially fast, but I felt strong.

CHAPTER THIRTEEN

It was Valentine's Day 2012, a couple of days after I had started at BuzzFeed, and from my desk in the middle of the open-plan office I could hear a commotion at the reception desk. Just then, we got an email with an exciting announcement: To celebrate Valentine's Day, BuzzFeed had gotten a white minihorse named Mystic to come hang out, and everyone was invited to take pictures. When I got to reception, I saw that the minihorse had a horn affixed to its head, so it looked like a unicorn, and ribbons on its mane. I bent down and someone took a picture, which I immediately posted to Instagram. If I was going to be working for the ultimate millennial startup, I might as well try to play the part.

The atmosphere at BuzzFeed could not have been more different than what I'd just come from at *Rolling Stone*. I'd been one of the younger employees at *Rolling Stone;* here, I was one of the oldest. BuzzFeed had a kitchen full of snacks and free soda and seltzer; at *Rolling Stone,* you had to pay a quarter to get a handful of peanut M&Ms from a gumball machine in the break room, which was too small to actually take a break in.

I was employee number sixty-five at BuzzFeed. Every other Thursday afternoon, the entire company would gather in the office kitchen for "BuzzFeed Brews," where we would eat pizza, drink beer, and welcome any new employees. All the new employees had to give a "fun fact" about themselves, in front of the whole company. Then Jonah Peretti, the company's CEO, would usually make an announcement about a new initiative or hand the microphone over to a department head to explain what their team had recently accomplished.

Every week there were at least five new hires, often more. When I started, the company had just gotten $15 million in new venture capital funding, and we had a mandate to grow—quickly. Jonah was determined to create a news division from scratch that would compete with big mainstream media outlets like *The New York Times.* Until very recently, BuzzFeed had been known for highlighting and creating viral online content, as well as for so-called native advertising, which from what I could tell basically consisted of posts paid for by big companies that were designed to be nearly indistinguishable from non-paid posts. Jonah was convinced that news content could also go viral, and that we'd be able to apply everything BuzzFeed had learned about creating "fun" viral content to news.

At *Rolling Stone,* I'd been a senior editor, which sounded like a more important job than it actually was. But now, I was running shit, and it was exciting. Sometimes I couldn't totally believe that this was my job: Ben put me in charge of creating an entertainment and lifestyle division. Jonah wanted Buzz-Feed to have a women-focused section to compete with blogs like Jezebel. I could launch sections for food, music, entertainment, sports. I'd never had the chance to create something like this from scratch, and I was very aware that it might never happen again—mostly because it's almost unheard of for a media company to just say, *Here's some money, just build something.* Usually when they say that, there's a catch, but as far as I could tell, there wasn't one this time. I didn't want to fuck it up.

Ben gave me pretty much carte blanche to hire as many people as I thought I needed. I'd never really hired anyone before, and there was just one overworked recruiter to give me guidance, so I operated mostly on instinct—if someone seemed smart and like they had good ideas, their references were decent, and Ben liked them, I usually took it on faith that they'd be a good employee. Sometimes this worked out, and sometimes it didn't. For senior positions, we'd often reach out to people in the industry we thought would be good, and they usually would come to a meeting at the office and then tell us they weren't interested. But a few times, we got approached by people who wanted to work for us whom I'd had a bad experience with, or who had a bad reputation. "We can't hire anyone gross," I said to Ben firmly, after he floated the name of a guy I'd worked with who had a reputation for preying on interns. But even guys with decent reputations seemed threatened by the notion of a woman in a position of power. Sometimes I'd be hiring for a job, and a man—it was always a man—would try to go around me and approach Ben; eventually I realized that these men had literally *never worked for a woman before.* To Ben's credit, he always responded, and CC'd me, saying that I was the one hiring for the job and would be in touch if I was interested.

I liked working for Ben, even if we were both kind of making things up as we went along. He had been a politics blogger, so he worked quickly and had sharp instincts for a good story, and he was excited about practically every idea I brought to him about expanding lifestyle and culture coverage. He was quirky—his phone was practically attached to his hand, and in meetings, if someone else was talking, he would just sit there scrolling Twitter and responding to emails, every so often making a comment without looking up from his phone. He wandered the newsroom, chatting with reporters constantly, as though he missed being one of them. Despite giving the okay for the teams in my purview, he also had little to no interest in those subject areas. Which was mostly fine, when he would leave us alone, except that sometimes he would suddenly get interested in them—usually when he felt like they weren't a big enough part of "the conversation." From what I could tell, "the conversation" consisted of the people Ben followed on Twitter, most of whom were politics and local New York news reporters.

Over the summer, Jonah decided he wanted to start covering the entertainment industry and simultaneously launch a video division that would create entertainment. I went out to Los Angeles to start trying to hire people to cover the industry. I'd been to L.A. several times before, but always for vacation or to visit friends, and it felt different and more important, somehow, to be going out there for work. L.A. felt exciting, romantic, new—and sunny. I stayed at the Sunset Tower Hotel, the classic Old Hollywood hotel on Sunset Boulevard that was also known as the site of the *Vanity Fair* Oscar party. One day, after a morning spent in my room doing work, I went downstairs for a meeting by the pool, which has a large patio for dining and a breathtaking view of Los Angeles. The weather was perfect—not too hot, the bright blue sky punctuated by palm trees. As I took in the view and waited for my appointment to arrive, I noticed a group of guys on a couch on the nearly empty patio, drinks and some food on the low table in front of them. It was the former *Entourage* star Kevin Connolly and a few of his friends, just casually hanging out on a weekday afternoon. This poolside C-list celebrity encounter was perfectly, deliciously on the nose, and I was enamored with all of it.

MEANWHILE, THE 2012 marathon was approaching. As the summer came to an end, I decided to stop drinking for the last couple of months of my training. I was proud of my newfound ability to run over the Brooklyn Bridge into Lower Manhattan and then run another seven or eight miles up the Hudson River path, and then back. My brother and sister-in-law, who lived close to the marathon route on the Upper East Side, offered to host my friends for brunch and then everyone could go cheer me on. My parents were going to come down from Boston; my sister from Washington, D.C. I felt loved and supported in what was about to be one of the biggest undertakings of my life. Sure, it wasn't a wedding or a pregnancy, but it was officially a big deal and I was glad it was being recognized.

I could hardly believe it: Just two and a half years earlier, I could barely run a mile, and now I was going to run a marathon. It became a point of pride for me, something that I didn't hesitate to tell people and wait for their disbelieving reactions. It was a new aspect to my identity that I had never thought I'd have, and I was loving it.

And then there was a storm. Hurricane Sandy was going to sweep up the East Coast and hit New York in the last week of

October. The night Sandy hit, I sat alone in my apartment in Fort Greene, watching the rain come down in sheets outside my window and listening to the wind howl. I'd bought a three-pound pork butt that I was planning on putting in the slow cooker the next morning; I may have been left to ride out the storm alone, but I'd have enough slow-cooked pork butt to last me for weeks. (It never crossed my mind to get other, possibly *slightly* more useful supplies, like batteries or bottled water.) At some point during the night, my internet went out, but I never lost power, and when I woke up the next morning, the internet was back. So while things in my neighborhood had never gotten especially bad, it wasn't immediately clear how devastated other parts of New York were. I put my pork butt in the slow cooker and settled in for the day.

It turned out that things elsewhere had gotten bad. *Really* bad. Huge swaths of the city had lost power, including the BuzzFeed office, and the subway shut down because the East River tunnels had flooded. BuzzFeed set up a spreadsheet so that people who still had power and internet (me!) could host our co-workers for the day; a lovely woman I'd never met before who worked on the product team came over. We sat at my dining room table (which doubled as my desk), but we didn't get much work done. I was glued to Twitter, impatient for any news of what was going on in the rest of the city. It looked like parts of Staten Island were basically under water, and people were missing. I looked around my cozy apartment, now infused with the scent of a slow-cooking pork butt, and felt a tinge of survivor's guilt.

In the first few days after Sandy hit, it seemed like the marathon, scheduled for that Sunday, would still happen. They couldn't cancel the *marathon*, could they? But then the number of people who had died during the storm started coming out—and it was shocking. So many people, many of them old and/or disabled, had drowned in their homes. And as the days went on, and the electricity and the subway still hadn't returned, it started to seem superficial to even care about the marathon at all. Many residents of city housing projects didn't have heat or power, and increasingly desperate calls for supplies went out on social media. I went to the Old Navy store near my house and bought a bunch of fleece sweatshirts and blankets and took them to a neighborhood organization in Red Hook that was distributing them to freezing residents.

For a couple of days, BuzzFeed set up a temporary office in the Hearst Building in Midtown, which still had power. (Hearst was a BuzzFeed investor.) There were buses leaving from the Barclays Center near my apartment to get into Manhattan, so I joined the long line and got on the bus to go over the Manhattan Bridge. Driving through the streets was eerie; the traffic lights were out, and cops were directing traffic at busy intersections. The streets felt empty. I was reminded of the disaster movie *I Am Legend,* particularly the scene where (uh, spoiler for a nearly fifteen-year-old movie coming up!) Will Smith's wife and child die in a helicopter crash as they're trying to escape Manhattan after the bridges and tunnels are shut down. That scene had always seriously freaked me out.

After work, I decided to head to Chelsea. For the past few months, I had been walking a miniature poodle named Sugar that belonged to an elderly, mostly housebound woman, and when I wasn't able to reach her on the phone, I figured I should go check on her.

Nancy lived in a large, institutional-like building that was a typical New York mix of older rent-stabilized tenants and twentysomethings who looked like they worked in finance. All of Lower Manhattan still didn't have electricity, and as I walked the thirty or so blocks to her apartment, I noticed that the typical buzz of the city had gone silent. Her building was likewise completely dark; the doorman had a flashlight and seemed nervous when I approached. "I'm here to see Nancy," I said, and he waved me up. I went up the stairs, the flashlight I had brought lighting the way, and made my way down the dark hallway. I knocked on her door. "Who is it?" she said, and I could hear fear in her voice.

"It's Doree," I said. "I came by to check on you. I tried calling you, but I guess you haven't been able to charge your phone."

She opened the door. The studio apartment was completely dark. It smelled of pee. "How are you doing?" I asked, even though it was obvious: not well.

"We're okay," she said.

"Do you want me to take Sugar out?" I asked. "Oh also— I brought you a flashlight." I hadn't been planning on giving the flashlight to her, but I couldn't handle seeing her sitting in the dark.

"No, you don't have to take him out," she said.

I was quiet for a moment. "Do you need anything? Do you need food? Can I go grocery shopping for you?"

"No, no," she said. "Thanks for coming by."

I left, feeling unsettled. I had a vision of myself, growing old and sitting in the dark in a New York studio apartment, alone. It scared me.

. . .

TWO DAYS BEFORE the marathon, it was still scheduled to happen. I went to the Javits Center, the huge convention center on the West Side Highway, to pick up my registration. It was a cloudy day, but not too cold; as I left and crossed Eleventh Avenue, carrying the bag holding my bright orange Marathon 2012 shirt, I saw on Twitter that the race had been canceled. I had been expecting it, but it still felt like a blow. All the training, the goals I'd set for myself—everything was gone. I didn't know how to process my disappointment. It still felt surreal, and it was also compounded by the fact that as the week had worn on, and the city had dithered about whether to go forward with the race, I had grown more and more wary of running it. The thought of running through neighborhoods that had been devastated by flooding, where people had died sitting in their homes—it felt wrong. The marathon was supposed to be a big, celebratory event, everyone's favorite New York City day, when people line the streets and cheer on the thousands of runners. Bands performed, people danced—it was a big, citywide party. It wouldn't be right to hold it right now.

I tried to find space to hold both of these competing feelings: that it was right to cancel, and that I was abjectly, horribly disappointed. I had a suspicion that I only had it in me to train for a marathon once in my life, and this had been my shot: a period where I wasn't dating anyone seriously, had no kids, wasn't drinking, had time to train, and was in reasonably good shape.

For weeks, I couldn't get up the motivation to run again.

When I finally did, I felt off, like it had been a completely different person who had been doing all that training for the past two years.

I went to see Cynthia, my therapist.

"I'm just having trouble wrapping my head around the fact that I trained for so long, and worked so hard, and then it just didn't happen," I said. "But I also feel guilty for feeling that way because I know so many people have it so much worse than me. Like, who cares about the dumb marathon? People died! People lost their homes!"

"You're still allowed to grieve the loss of the marathon," Cynthia said. "It was something you worked really hard for."

"I think I also just feel like, after all the bullshit with Luke and everything else, that this was a sort of salvation," I said. "Like running the marathon would be a way I could definitively move on."

"That makes sense," she said. "I don't think you need to feel guilty about that."

"I'm just questioning whether I even want to stay in New York," I said. "Sandy was so grim, my apartment has mice that I can hear in the walls. And my dating life is so grim too."

"You're not alone; I hear a lot of my female clients say that about dating in New York," Cynthia said. "It's really hard."

"It just feels like the odds are not in my favor," I said, warming to my topic. "The few guys who are single and who I'd potentially be interested in have literally dozens if not hundreds of women just like me to choose from—smart, reasonably attractive, work in media, listen to the same bands, read the same books. I feel like I see my literal clones everywhere." I paused. I'd never quite articulated it this way, not even to myself. "And every time I do go on a date it's just depressing. It honestly feels hopeless."

It didn't help that at BuzzFeed, it seemed like all my co-workers in their twenties were hooking up with each other. I certainly didn't want to hook up with any of them (not to mention I was determined never to date anyone I worked with ever again), but it just underscored how I felt like I was aging out of my opportunities to meet anyone. I knew on a rational level that certainly not every person who didn't get married ended up like Nancy, alone in the dark in an apartment that smelled of dog pee, with no family or friends to help her. And I also knew that getting married was certainly no guarantee that I wouldn't end up alone. But another part of me couldn't stop thinking about Nancy as she sat in the darkness of her apartment; my mind was drawing a straight line between "goes on a bunch of mediocre OkCupid dates" and "lives alone in sad apartment, dies." And it felt like if I *did* want to meet someone and get married, it was not going to be in New York.

"I just feel like I want my life to be . . . easier," I said to Cynthia. "Is that a bad thing?"

CHAPTER FOURTEEN

I was in L.A. for three weeks to help solidify the new Buzz-Feed L.A. bureau, but also to test the waters about whether I wanted to live there. I had rented a MINI Cooper, perfect for squeezing into tight street parking spots in Los Feliz, the neighborhood where I was staying, and I'd told everyone I knew in Los Angeles that I'd be in town.

The second night I was there, I met up with my friend Lara, her husband, and a bunch of their friends at a bar in the neighborhood; Lara was also visiting from out of town, but her husband used to live in L.A., and between the two of them they knew a lot of people. I started talking to a friendly blond woman named Steph who, it turned out, had moved from New York to L.A. just a couple of months before.

"We *love* it here," she said. "We live around the corner. It's so nice. I was living in a shitty apartment in Williamsburg and I haven't looked back."

We'd been talking for half an hour or so when I finally put it together who she was: a hilarious writer I already followed on Twitter. "You're *that* Steph!" I exclaimed. "I've followed you on Twitter forever. You're so funny."

"I obviously think you should move here," Steph said. "How long are you in town for? Do you want to come over and watch movies sometime this week?" I left the bar feeling buoyant. Friends! I didn't even live here yet, and I was making friends.

A few days later, I hung out with my friend Scott, and on our way home we stopped at a Whole Foods in Pasadena to get a snack. I hadn't even realized how inured I'd become to the experience of going to a grocery store in New York—the long lines, the crowded aisles, the cramped stores—until I saw this literal palace of a supermarket. It seemed *enormous*, with beautiful produce (in January!), more aisles than I'd ever seen, and almost no line to check out. I wandered the aisles. Everything looked shiny, colorful, gleaming, pristine, abundant. It was like I was seeing food for the first time.

I'd been so enamored with New York, both before and while I lived there. I had pictured myself as a kind of grown-up Harriet, sharp and sophisticated, feeling like the city and I were intertwined. Even though I wasn't from New York, and there was no real reason why I should feel more attached to that city than anywhere else, New York has a way of sinking its tentacles into you and it's really, really hard to shake. For so long, my whole sense of self had been wrapped up in being someone who lived in New York. Who was I, if I didn't live there?

When I left my PhD program, I feared that quitting meant that I was a failure. I felt similarly about leaving New York, that it would mean I wasn't tough enough or hardened enough or *strong* enough to live there, that the city had finally worn me down and now I was at the point where it didn't take much more than a *Whole Foods* to get me to move—how *embarrass-*

ing. I was enticed by the sunny (read: shallow) openness of the West Coast, just like millions of apparently weak people before me had been. I would just be the living embodiment of another "Why I Left New York" essay, mercilessly mocked across the internet.

I was more worried about how people would react to my decision to leave than whether I actually wanted to leave in the first place. Why did I overlay every decision with the fear of being judged? I needed to do what was right for *me*, not what I thought people wanted or expected me to do. It had never been clearer to me that I needed a new start.

I FINALLY MADE the decision to go to L.A. New York would always be here; I could always come back. But even as I made the plans to move—booking the movers, buying a plane ticket, having one last tag sale to get rid of stuff from my apartment— I felt a seed of doubt planting itself in my mind. Wasn't I getting a little old for new starts? Wasn't part of being an adult learning how to stick things out, not abandoning ship anytime things got hard? I tried to ignore it. This wasn't a sign of being a quitter, or giving up. This was actually a sign of adulthood, I decided. I could finally recognize my needs and act on them, and not have to wait for anyone to give me permission.

I had a big going-away party at a bar near my house, and I stumbled home, drunk on Negronis and nostalgia, at two in the morning, stopping at a bodega on Fulton Street so I could get a two-dollar fried chicken drumstick. I ate it as I walked, the grease dripping down my chin.

PART TWO

CHAPTER FIFTEEN

The apartment building was on a quiet street not far from the Grove, the outdoor L.A. shopping mall where people— maybe tourists, maybe not?—like to take photos in front of its gaudy Italianate fountain, which plays music and does a "show" every fifteen minutes or so, like a junior varsity Bellagio. It was the fifth or so apartment I had seen in two days, and I was starting to get anxious about finding a place in L.A., since I was supposed to be moving in three weeks.

But as soon as the landlord led me into the courtyard, I felt like I didn't even need to see the apartment itself; I knew this was the one. It was a Spanish-style building, with each of the eight apartments' windows facing the exterior or the courtyard. The courtyard itself was lush and calm, with a small fountain with a very small stream of water bubbling through it. I was enchanted.

"So you know, Elisabeth Shue and Davis Guggenheim used to live in the apartment downstairs from this one," the landlord said as he opened the door to the apartment in the back corner of the courtyard, name-dropping the actress and her director husband. "And when they were rebooting *Melrose*

Place, he wanted to shoot the pilot here, but it didn't work out." I had no particular affinity for either Davis Guggenheim or Elisabeth Shue, but he had correctly pegged me as someone who would be impressed by a tenuous connection to Hollywood fame. I was quickly learning that in L.A., almost everything has a tenuous connection to Hollywood fame.

We walked into the living room. The walls were painted white but instead of feeling blank and utilitarian, the room radiated lightness. Sun dappled the hardwood floors, and archways led to the dining room and the hallway. Casement windows, stretching to the ceiling, overlooked the courtyard. The bedroom was enormous, light and airy; there was a washer and dryer off the kitchen, and a back door that led to a little patio and a set of stairs. "Davis wanted to paint the doors to shoot the pilot, but my mom said no. And Bebe Neuwirth lived here for five years." More Hollywood!

"Here?" I asked, opening the kitchen cabinets and drawers. They looked original. No dishwasher, I noted, but that would be fine. I'd have so much *space*—the apartment felt like it was double the size of my place in Brooklyn. I started picturing where I would put everything—the dining room could double as an office, and in the living room, I could get a small sleeper sofa for all the out-of-town guests who'd probably want to come visit immediately. I'd keep the bedroom pretty spare, I thought, probably just a bed and maybe an armoire, because the closet space was tight, and get some sheer curtains to let the light in.

"Yup," he said. "*In this apartment.*"

It seemed *so* L.A.—a romantic, beautiful apartment that had formerly been occupied by a well-known actress, with another well-known actress and her director husband who used to live downstairs. Never mind that no one famous lived here now; it was the history that mattered, so when I told people back in New York where I was living, they would be suitably impressed. I felt like I needed to fulfill their fantasy of L.A., as well as mine. And besides, I didn't yet know that almost every older apartment in Los Angeles has had *someone* at least semi-famous living in it.

WHEN I MOVED to L.A. in 2013, I was more than ready to start a new chapter, and so I decided: I would say yes to everything. I'd gotten too comfortable with my insular media world in New York; it had been too easy to go to all the same parties where I saw all the same people, get into the same routines, eat at the same restaurants, and drink at the same bars. So I threw myself into my new life. I went to open gallery nights, I went to dinner parties with people I barely knew. I spent Saturday afternoons hiking. Was I losing my jaded New Yorker–ness in my newfound lust for life? I wouldn't go *that* far, but I was, actually, enjoying myself.

I also tried to broaden my dating horizons. I went out with a children's social worker who took me on bike trips all over L.A. County, but who was very cheap in a way that I had initially chalked up to environmentalism (he didn't use paper towels!) but turned out to just be an allergy to spending money on anything besides weed. He was also a terrible driver. He drove his Toyota SUV leaning forward, almost hunched over the steering wheel, and way too fast, with a nervous energy. One sunny weekend morning, we headed out from his apartment to go on a bike ride in the Apple Valley, about an hour and a half out of town. As he sped along the 10 Freeway cursing at drivers, switching lanes without signaling, and cutting people off, I clutched the passenger-side door, praying that we'd make it back alive.

I realized you could learn a lot about guys based on what and how they drove, a piece of data, as Cynthia might say, that had not been available to me in New York. (That said, I preferred accumulating that data while not being terrified I was going to die in a fiery car crash on the 10 with a guy who snored so loudly I'd once had to sneak out of his house in the middle of the night.)

Car culture was another new aspect of my life in L.A., and I embraced it in true New York transplant fashion: I leased a convertible. I loved the idea of driving around the city, top down, sun shining. When it came time to actually get the car, my friend Michael, another BuzzFeed reporter who'd recently moved to L.A., accompanied me to the Volvo dealership in Culver City. Michael was also all about his new L.A. life; he'd bought a shiny silver Mercedes coupe and rented an apartment in the Hollywood Hills. "You *gotta* get the convertible," he said. His bright blue eyes were shining. "It's *perfect*." The convertible was a Volvo C70, the last year they'd be making this car. We sat in the salesman's office as he went over the lease terms. "Take it!" Michael urged me.

"Can you get the total payment down a bit?" I asked. The salesman could. I was sold. Michael high-fived me on the way out. Never mind that I was almost thirty-six and buying (well, leasing) a car for the very first time—I felt accomplished, grown-up.

The car I'd selected—black on black—wasn't in stock, so the dealership gave me a loaner car that was the same model, in baby blue with a white leather interior, a car that looked like

I was on my way to my weekly canasta game with the gals. When I drove the car home, I immediately encountered a problem. My building had a carport in the back, and each apartment had an assigned parking space. Mine was in the middle, and there was very little space between the garage and the building. I felt my hands get clammy as I attempted to maneuver the car into the space. Then I heard a sickening crunch. While dripping with beautiful period details, vintage Los Angeles apartments were built at a time when cars were much smaller, and thus, the garages and carports in these buildings were also tiny—a seemingly minor detail that I, who had never parked a car in a garage before, had overlooked. I *might* have been okay if I still had the MINI Cooper I had driven around on my initial visit, but this car was substantially bigger.

"Fucking A," I said as I got out to survey the damage. The only small consolation was that I had scraped it along a wall of the carport, and not damaged the car in the spot next to mine. But still. I had broken the mirror and put a long gouge in the passenger-side door. I'd had the car for approximately two hours.

I *wanted* to be the kind of person who says, "Let's go for a drive!" and puts on her leather driving gloves and red lipstick and huge sunglasses and silk kerchief and slides behind the wheel of her 1966 Ford Thunderbird with her best friend, like Thelma and/or Louise, minus the attempted rape and the whole thing about driving off a precipice in the Grand Canyon. But in reality, I recalled that during brief periods of my life when I'd had access to cars, it had been a disaster: I scraped the sides on walls, dented them, crashed into fences, sideswiped other drivers, and took my passenger-side mirror off because I'd miscalculated the distance between my car and a gate, just to name a few of my priors. My driving debacles went back to my driver's test when I was sixteen. It had just snowed, and some streets were still unplowed in Somerville, where I was taking the test. The state trooper giving me the driving test told me to drive up and over a steep hill, but I miscalculated where to stop at the top, and the car started sliding slowly down the hill. Somehow, I still passed.*

The accident in the loaner car seemed like a bad omen. But a couple of days later, when my actual car got delivered, I slid into it and pushed the button to make the top go down, and up, and down, and up, over and over again. I would put the accident behind me and embrace the new car—and my new life. But I also decided that I would park on the street.

A COUPLE OF months after I moved to L.A., I turned thirty-six. I celebrated with a housewarming-slash-birthday party at my new apartment; my sister flew in from D.C. to celebrate with me. "Your apartment is gorgeous!" people said, one after the other, as they came in, and then I turned around and the apartment was packed. I had friends! These friends were pouring themselves drinks and admiring the art on the walls! I remembered the conversation I'd had with my former Gawker co-worker Alex, when he'd warned me about breaking up with Jon and being, at minimum, thirty-six before I'd be having a

---

* Three years later, the same state trooper was arrested for participating in a scheme to sell drivers' licenses to undocumented immigrants, which made his comment during our test that he was "happy to be testing someone who spoke English" not just racist, but ironic.

kid. But here I was, thirty-six and single, and yet somehow feeling calmer about my situation than ever before. I may not have been married, but I was figuring out what a fulfilled life meant—on my own terms.

Maybe I'd needed to get out of New York in order to see that clearly. For so long, I'd been so focused on getting the approval of everyone else, men especially, and trying to make myself into someone that other people would like, that I'd completely ignored what and who *I* actually liked. And now, I was ready for this to change.

CHAPTER SIXTEEN

In college, I was friends with a guy named Phil who lived upstairs from me in our freshman dorm. Phil was a charming, preppy weirdo who often wore an ascot to eat dinner in the dining hall. He also loved to party. For Spring Fling, he installed an inflatable pool in his single room and filled it with a hose connected to his sink and invited friends to sit in the pool and drink beer. Unfortunately, he lived directly above our RA, and when water started dripping into her room through the ceiling, the pool had to be deflated. He became a ubiquitous presence at my school's parties—frat parties, underground parties, cocktail parties. You name it, Phil was there. Years later, I was out one night with him and a few other friends, and the conversation turned to how Phil hit on women. "If I'm at a bar, maybe I'll talk to twenty women in a night, okay?" he said. "Nineteen of them will blow me off, but there's usually one who I'll hook up with."

"*What?*" I said. I couldn't believe what I was hearing, laid out so starkly like this.

He laughed and said, "It's really just a numbers game."

I was horrified by this on a few levels: by the sheer energy required to approach so many people, by the cold-blooded approach to dating, by his view of women as essentially interchangeable, and most of all by the idea of being rejected nineteen times in one night. If I got rejected *once* in a night it was enough to send me into a self-loathing spiral. But it didn't seem to faze Phil at all. He didn't take it personally; he knew he wasn't everyone's cup of tea, but he also knew that the reasons a woman might not want to talk to or hook up with him on any particular night didn't necessarily have to do with *him*. Maybe she had a boyfriend, maybe she was tired, maybe she had a crush on someone else, maybe she wasn't interested in men, maybe he had inadvertently said something that rubbed her the wrong way. It didn't matter; he didn't dwell on it. He moved on.

This felt like an approach to dating that was probably only physically safe for male-identified people to do. Plus, when a woman approaches multiple men in a bar, she's assumed to be a sex worker and/or "desperate," but when a guy does it, it's just guys being guys. Thanks, patriarchy. But when I got to L.A., I realized I didn't need to try to hit on dozens of men in bars every night. Instead, I allowed myself to stop thinking that every guy I went out with *had* to have soul mate potential. I could say yes to guys I might not have given a second glance in the past. And besides, maybe I'd had too narrow a definition of the kind of guy I "should" be with: I didn't necessarily have a *visual* ideal, but it felt like a deal breaker if a guy misspelled a word on his OkCupid profile, or posted with a fish he'd just caught in one of his photos. Not just because I thought he needed to look "good on paper," but because I had assumed that I wouldn't have anything in common with someone who spent his weekends on a river. But maybe my perfect match was hiding behind what seemed to me to be imperfections. Maybe I was supposed to be with a grammatically imperfect fly fisherman!

Then I remembered I had a friend, Tamara, who had basically done exactly this. After she turned thirty-one, she had gone on thirty-one dates in thirty-one days, and ended up meeting her now-husband on one of these dates. She even wrote a book about it, *31 Dates in 31 Days*. Yes, it was a gimmick, but there was something about it that had worked. Maybe there *was* something to the idea that quantity influences quality. I didn't want to go on a date every day for thirty-one days, but I *did* want to start dating a lot more than I had been. Maybe dating a wide variety of guys would help me figure out exactly what I was looking for.

A THING I quickly picked up about living in L.A. is that everyone makes fun of *The Secret,* the book about the law of attraction, which basically says that you can will things to happen for you by changing your thoughts and "putting things out into the universe." But even though it's widely mocked, I started to encounter a lot of people—even other former jaded New Yorkers!—who kind of believed that *The Secret* was real. Of course, the lessons of *The Secret* aren't new. L.A. has a long tradition of religions, cults, and self-help organizations like Scientology, Landmark Forum, and EST that all traffic in the belief that we are in charge of our own destiny and that we have the power to "speak things into reality," and they are an outgrowth of a uniquely American bootstrap, individualist mentality that is skeptical of little things like, I don't know, mental health struggles, structural inequality, systemic racism, and the centrifugal economic inequalities of capitalism that *just may* contribute to some people not becoming gajillionaires by the time they're twenty-five—or even just having a job that pays the rent. But without even really realizing it, I started picking up on this vocabulary, too.

"I really want to meet someone," I told my friend Gabrielle over brunch. I had typically shied away from announcing my intentions so baldly—I had previously thought that it meant you were a sad, desperate, lonely person if you actually articulated that you wanted to meet someone. Now, though, I realized that not only was it okay to be all those things, but also that being single didn't mean that you were sad, desperate, and lonely, and it was *also* okay to let people know that you wanted to be in a relationship. I added, "I'm just putting it out into the universe."

"Hmm," she said. "Have you heard of Tinder? It's a new dating app my friend told me about." She pulled out her phone. "It started on college campuses, so it's a lot of really young guys, but it's still kind of cool." She opened the app and showed me. "It just shows you guys' pictures with a short description, and then you swipe left or right on them. Left for no, right for yes. And if they also swipe right on you, then you 'match' and you can contact each other."

In my online dating life, I'd mostly used OkCupid, which sometimes seemed overly concerned with making exact matches. It had you take surveys that asked questions ranging from "Would you date someone who kept a gun in the house?" to "What is your opinion of sarcasm?" and then based your percentage match with someone on how you'd answered the questions and what you said you were looking for in a partner. The result was that I matched with a lot of guys who were a lot like me: highly educated, often working in media, with the exact same outlook and interests and goals. There was comfort in this, but I was also wary. Was my perfect partner someone I matched with at 99 percent, or was that *too* similar and I should be looking for a match that was more like, say, 85 percent? It was too easy to become obsessed with these numbers, to think that an algorithm could instantly spit out the perfect partner if you both said you believed that dinosaurs had never existed (to be fair, I didn't want to date someone who didn't believe in evolution, but this also felt like a pretty low bar).

I also felt like OkCupid encouraged people to write long emails, which I found time-consuming and tiring to read and respond to. It's one thing to be clever and flirty over text with someone you've never met, but another to be clever and flirty over a five-hundred-word email with a total stranger. I called these guys pen pals—they weren't actually interested in going on a date; they just wanted someone to dump all their thoughts and feelings on.

So Tinder intrigued me, because it eliminated all pretense of trying to match people based on preferences or beliefs or desires. You could tell the app where you were interested in dating people, how old you wanted them to be, and if you had a sex or gender preference. And that was it. The immediacy and the gut instinct appealed to me. I could see how it could be construed as superficial, because so much emphasis was placed on photos. But having been dating online for a while now, I knew that people revealed a lot, intentionally or otherwise, in the photos they chose for their online dating profile. I still didn't think I was a "guy who is posing with a fish they just caught" lady, but was I a "shirtless guy doing a handstand on Venice Beach" or a "guy in front of a microphone doing stand-up" kind of gal? These were types of guys I hadn't encountered in New York, where the men were easily categorizable in buckets like finance bro and media nerd. Where did I fit in in this new dating taxonomy? Maybe I wasn't either a shirtless handstand person *or* a stand-up comedy person. And also, Tinder didn't solve the fundamental dating app predicament: What if no one liked me?

In keeping with my whole new saying-yes-to-everything philosophy, I went out with a very, shall we say, *wide* range of people, and because I was new in town, I usually deferred to them when it came time to plan our dates. There was the children's social worker, but there was also an Orthodox Jew who installed AV equipment for a living and liked to go to Vegas with his buddies and hole up in his hotel room on Shabbat with kosher food he'd brought from home, and who took me to a secret live acoustic show where Chris Martin was performing. (I think I failed to act suitably impressed by this, because he ghosted me not long after.) There was the guy from Orange County, who seemed uncomfortable the whole dinner and told me that one of the main reasons he liked living in Orange County was there was so much more parking; a newspaper editor I'd met at the BuzzFeed L.A. launch party back in November who never texted me back after going camping in the Sequoia National Forest (he's alive, I checked); a sweet guy who worked in digital media who took me to an improv show at UCB; a TV writer who knew a bunch of people I knew in New York who took me to a fancy Mexican restaurant; a quiet guy who took me for amazing fish tacos at a restaurant near the airport; a guy who went to a museum exhibit with me at LACMA; a guy who played the piano; an agent who took me for drinks at a hotel in Beverly Hills; a guy who was a good sport about running into some of my friends on a first date; and a guy who hit me up for a job at BuzzFeed after we had a mediocre date at a wine bar near my house. There also was an ex–Orthodox Jew who was a truck driver, and a guy whose brother was a famous actor. I even went out with Marc Anthony's touring bassist.

I found that I had to keep two competing thoughts in my head before each date. One was: It's just a date, it probably won't go anywhere and that's fine, just relax and have fun. The other was allowing myself to get excited about the dates: picking out my outfit, doing my hair, making sure my lip gloss wasn't on my teeth, spritzing just a smidge of Chloe Eau de Parfum on my wrists. (I drew the line at bikini waxes, though. If I ended up sleeping with a date, he was just going to have to be okay with whatever I had going on down there.) And then a funny thing started happening as I was going on all these dates: I started worrying less about whether the guy I was on a date with liked me, and more about whether I liked *him*. As I went on more and more dates, the stakes for each subsequent date didn't feel quite so high, and I was able to relax and be myself more. And I was able to recognize when a guy just wasn't right for me. Maybe *The Secret* wasn't anything mystical or magical—maybe it was just the not-so-revolutionary-but-sometimes-impossible concept of knowing yourself well enough to know what you want. (Which, I should add, is different than the old dating cliché that you need to "love yourself first" before anyone else can.)

I thought about all the energy I'd spent worrying about whether Luke liked me, or if he liked me, did he *really* like me, and if he *really* liked me . . . It was just a never-ending spiral of needing more and more validation, but I barely ever stopped to think about whether he was giving *me* what I needed.

But now I could feel things changing. Take this one guy, Josh, whom I'd had a nice dinner with at an Italian restaurant near my apartment. We'd kissed, and then I didn't hear from him, and eventually he texted me to say that he really enjoyed meeting me but he'd gotten back together with someone. *No worries,* I thought. But then, he resurfaced a few months later and said that he had regretted not going out with me again, that the other woman hadn't worked out, and could we go out again?

I wasn't especially physically attracted to him, but I figured, what the hell. Year of yes! And he seemed kind and sweet, the type of guy for whom I thought maybe an attraction could evolve. So I went out with him, and we ended up back at his apartment. He played piano, and we sat at his piano and sang for a while, which was fun, and then had pretty forgettable sex, which was not. In the morning, I woke up and realized: *This guy is lovely, but not for me.* He asked if I wanted to get breakfast and I said I had to go, and then I told him that I didn't think it was going to work out between us. But afterward, Josh was persistent—he called and texted, and told me he really liked me. Past Me would have buckled at this point because the idea of someone I could tolerate who was *really* into me was too alluring. But truly, Josh was not right for me.

Or take Marc Anthony's bassist. We went on a daytime date at a bar in Los Feliz, and he was charming and cute and smart, and at the end of the date said he wanted to hang out again, and I agreed. But then a game of text tag ensued: Most days he was only available late at night, like after eleven P.M., and then he wasn't available on the weekends because he was rehearsing or traveling. Instead of bending over backward to try to figure out a time that worked, eventually I just gave up.

Even though I felt like I was becoming more confident and secure with myself, it still took a lot of mental energy to be *on* all the time in the way that dating requires. My friend Samantha—one of my only real friends at work—had similarly decided that she was tired of dating apps. "Let's go on a man cleanse," she said matter-of-factly, sitting across from me in my office one afternoon. "Like, it's not forever, but we just need to *detox*. Work on ourselves."

That was exactly it—I needed to detox. I was still trying to be open, to say yes to people I might have passed over previously, but the mechanics of online dating are basically equivalent to having a very busy part-time job and anyone who tries to tell you otherwise is straight-up lying or hasn't done it very much.*

First there was the actual matching with people. Then came messaging on the app, a back-and-forth where I was supposed to be witty and flirty and reveal just enough about myself to be interesting without saying too much in case the guy was a serial killer. Then if things were going well and I had determined

---

* Possibly worse are the long-married friends who met their partners when they were twenty-two who say things like, "Wow, I feel so lucky that I met Trent before dating apps existed! I'd be so bad at them!" It's just, like, no, actually, you probably would have figured them out like everyone else, and trust me, I am not particularly enthused about being on them either. These are also the friends who like to grab your phone and swipe for you and then say things like, "You weren't kidding! These guys *suck*!" If you have been one of these people, this is just a friendly note that this is *really fucking annoying*.

that he was in all likelihood *not* a serial killer, we'd switch to texting outside the app. I also preferred to have a phone call before I went on a date, because in the same way a single photo can be incredibly revealing, a single phone call could also tell me a lot about a person. Then there was the whole dance of deciding if I wanted to meet up with him and he with me and finally making plans, around 25 percent of which got canceled or postponed for one reason or another, getting my hopes up for said plans, and if we eventually, *finally* met up, it was often a letdown to realize that they were just . . . *fine*.

During the man cleanse, I started questioning what I was doing all of this for, anyway. What if marriage just wasn't right for me? I'd gone out with more than thirty people in the year since moving to L.A., not to mention all the people I'd dated in New York. And not *one* of them was right for me?

I started allowing myself to picture what my life would look like if I was single. I thought about what it would be like to spend holidays with my family and be the only one who wasn't married with children. Would I be pitied? And was I more concerned about being pitied than I actually was about being single? That is, was I more worried about what other people thought about my being single than *actually* being single? I wasn't sure.

Certainly, now, at almost thirty-seven, I felt like my window was starting to close, and I hated that I thought about it in terms of a "window." I was frustrated by how fixated I was on meeting someone, but part of me also wondered why I should feel shame about wanting to be in a relationship. Wanting love and companionship is a basic human need, and I felt that women, in particular, are framed as being "desperate" if we dared articulate that we actually wanted to get married, especially if we were in our late thirties or older. I wanted to reframe my thinking, to simultaneously be okay with the idea of being single while also allowing myself to articulate that I wanted to find a partner. Was it mental gymnastics? Perhaps. But it was the most honest I'd been with myself in a long time.

A COUPLE OF WEEKS after I had started my man cleanse, I had lunch at Son of a Gun, a trendy restaurant near my apartment, with my friend Heather, who writes the Ask Polly column for The Cut and is just as wise and perceptive in person as she is in her column. "So. Are you dating?" she asked. Heather is one of those long-married people who loves to discuss your dating life, which I normally found voyeuristic and annoying, but not from her—she was genuinely interested in dissecting what was going on.

"Eh," I said, picking at my lobster roll. I recalled that the last time I'd been to this restaurant I'd been on a date with fish taco guy, and I remembered that the conversation had been pleasant but stilted and that when I subsequently told him that I wasn't interested in seeing him again, he seemed insulted, as though he had wasted his time taking me out. "Not really. I went out with this guy who was the touring bassist for Marc Anthony, who was actually really interesting, and we had a good time and both wanted to hang out again, but it was basically impossible to schedule a second date because he was always rehearsing or performing, and he wanted to meet up at, like, eleven at night and I'm usually in bed by then! I can't be meeting someone for a date *at* eleven, like maybe we will stay out until eleven or even midnight, but does he think I'm twenty-two? Eleven is *way* too late to go on a date, I guess unless you work nights or something, which I don't."

I took a sip of water and continued. "So I texted him, 'Hey, I had a really great time with you and I was looking forward to hanging out again, but it seems like our schedules are just too difficult to sort out right now. Take care!' And I gotta say, as soon as I sent the text, I felt a weight lift. I feel like the old me would have gone above and beyond to try to hang out with this guy—I *would* have met up with him at eleven at night, or whenever he was around. I would have rearranged my life to accommodate his."

Heather smiled. "I think this is a *very* good thing," she said.

"You do?" I said. She seemed enthusiastic in a way I wasn't expecting.

"Yes," she said. "You knew what you needed out of a relationship, and even if you were attracted to this guy, you knew that it wasn't enough. And so you said goodbye." She looked at me, as though taking me in. "I'm telling you—this is *really* great."

"Well, thanks," I said. "Yeah, you know, now that you say it, I guess I kind of . . . took control of the situation."

She smiled again. "I have a feeling that this means you're about to meet someone you really like," she said. "It just feels that way. Like now you know what you want, and what you need, and that person is going to materialize."

"So you're saying *The Secret* works, then," I said.

"I'm just saying—*Secret* or not, I think you're finally ready to meet someone. Maybe you thought you were before, but now you *really* are."

CHAPTER SEVENTEEN

The man cleanse had cleared my head—it had been nice to not have to think about dating for a little while. During the cleanse, my friend Emily, my old Gawker co-worker, came to visit for a couple of days. She brought a housewarming gift with her: a tarot deck called the Wild Unknown. "I like to just draw a card every day," she said, showing me the cards and the book that revealed their meaning. "It's just kind of like, a guide for the day, something to focus on, how your day is going to go."

We had a great time—we went to a party hosted by a writer we both admired in the hills above Studio City, we sang karaoke downtown with a few other friends of Emily's who lived in L.A., and we ate delicious Japanese food. I was sad to see her go.

The morning after she left, I drew a card: the Ace of Cups. It represented love, joy, happiness, emotional fulfillment. I texted her a photo of it and wrote: "Feels auspicious."

"Holy shit!" she wrote back.

My auspicious tarot card draw notwithstanding, I was re-energized about getting back on the apps. I had a theory that when you deleted Tinder and then re-downloaded it, it gave you "better" options than it might have previously, and one of the first guys who popped up was named Matt who looked kind of familiar. I scrolled through his photos. He had a handsome, friendly face, a really nice smile, big brown eyes. He was holding a guitar in one of the photos. No photos of him with fish, or doing shirtless headstands, or in front of a microphone. His profile was charming and funny, but not in a way that said, *I'm funny, laugh at my jokes,* even though he was a comedy writer and was thus professional-level *funny* and *good at jokes.* Instead, it bragged self-deprecatingly about how he'd been quoted in his hometown newspaper in Massachusetts about the best lobster rolls. Oh! He was from Massachusetts. That was a bonus. My only reservation was that he was only thirty—a full six years younger than me. *Better a mature thirty than an immature forty,* I thought, and swiped right. I immediately got the notification that we had matched.

I got a message from him a few minutes later. "Hey, I've never used this app before so I'm not totally sure what I'm supposed to say, but hi." I rolled my eyes. I felt like guys claiming that they'd never been on the app before was a common opening salvo, meant to be disarming, and I debated simply not responding. But in the spirit of attempting to be more openminded, I messaged him back. We went back and forth a few times, then started texting, and then a couple of days later I asked if he wanted to talk on the phone. He did.

He called later that night. It turned out he worked on a late-night show on Comedy Central where my friend Steph also worked. It was a relief that he wasn't a total stranger, and talking to him felt so comfortable, like I'd known him for ages. He told me about his family—he was the youngest of four, and his next-oldest sibling was seven years older—and about coming to L.A. "I moved here when I was twenty-three because I wanted to write comedy," he said. "I didn't know anyone except my roommate." They lived in Pasadena, he said, and he'd applied to work at the Apple Store and at Starbucks, and the Apple Store got back to him first. So he'd become a Mac Genius at the Apple Store at the Grove and worked there for almost five years.

"Didn't you get discouraged?" I asked. "Five years is a long time."

"I had given myself five years to get a job in entertainment, and I did," he said.

"That's amazing," I said. I found Matt's self-made career extremely attractive. Hollywood is full of people whose parents have worked in the industry for decades, who got them their first jobs as production assistants or in the mailroom at an agency. Matt had done it all on his own, without even graduating from college. He explained that while he was working at the Apple Store, he met people, some of them famous, who'd brought their computers in to be serviced, and he started a podcast with one of them. Eight years later, he was still podcasting, he'd done a lot of stand-up, he'd been a host on a daily TV show, and now was a staff writer on a nightly game show on Comedy Central. I was impressed.

It wasn't just his résumé, though. There was something about the ease of our conversation that felt . . . different. And the way that he told me he was impressed with *my* job was also attractive. I'd gone on way too many dates where I belatedly realized that I had been subtly downplaying my accomplishments or my job because I thought that would make me more appealing. I hated that I had done that. So it was refreshing to feel like not only did I not have to downplay my own résumé, but also that it made me more attractive to Matt. It made me think he would celebrate my professional accomplishments, not feel like they threatened him in some way.

We went out for the first time a couple days later. It turned out he lived down the block from me, so we decided to go to a bar near both our apartments, and he walked over to pick me up. As I descended the stairs from my apartment, I saw him standing in the courtyard, beaming. He was beaming—at *me*! "You look really nice," he said, and I smiled.

"So do you," I said. He was very cute in person, with big brown eyes and a wide smile.

And he was easy to talk to, sweet and funny and disarmingly personal. "I worked in a funeral home for four years," he said. "My two best friends, they're brothers, their family owns a funeral home and so I worked there. I also worked in an ice cream shop and once almost got locked in the freezer and all I could think about was that the headline in the papers would be 'Fat Guy Dies in Ice Cream Shop.'" He saw my confused face—he wasn't skinny, but he didn't look fat, either—and added, "Oh, I lost a hundred pounds in the past year. In high school I weighed four hundred pounds, then I did gastric bypass surgery and lost weight, then gained some back, and then about a year ago I decided to start working out and eat better." He was matter-of-fact about this.

"Wow," I said. I thought back to the summer after Jon and I had broken up, when I became obsessive about exercise and everything I ate, and yet I had never moved through the world as a fat person—just as a straight-sized person who had internalized a lot of messaging about the "ideal" body.

We talked some more—about my family, and my job, and

living in Los Angeles, and then, perched on barstools, we kissed. I didn't even care that it was in front of the bartender.

Matt walked me home, and we kissed goodbye outside the door to my apartment. "When can we hang out again?" he said.

"Um . . . Friday?" I said. I usually tried to play it a little cooler. I'd also been burned by guys who seemed really eager at first, and then as soon as I showed real interest, they withdrew. So I was slightly wary, but I was also trying to listen to my gut, which was telling me that Matt was different. I was also more willing to take a risk I might not have before because I knew *I* liked him.

"Great," he said.

"You choose what we do," I told him. "I'm leaving it all in your hands." When it comes to activities, I'm a planner, which sometimes gets exhausting. I wanted to see if Matt could plan something, too.

THAT FRIDAY, Matt picked me up in his car. "So where are we going?" I said.

He grinned. "Disneyland."

"Okay, wow!" I said. I was into it, but I was a little skeptical—I wasn't someone who especially loved Disney, nor had I felt compelled to visit Disneyland since moving to L.A. "Is this a thing people do, go on dates to Disneyland?"

He looked at me from the driver's seat. "Yeah, of course," he said. "You don't need to have kids to go to Disneyland."

I knew that, of course, but I had always been confused by adults who went to Disneyland without kids. What was the point? But once we got there, I had to admit, it *did* feel pretty special. I took a photo of Sleeping Beauty's palace, which sits at the end of Main Street, all lit up. I posted it on Instagram and captioned it: "Typical Friday night hang." The night was fun and silly and we held hands as we walked around, and Matt introduced me to Dole Whip, and to cream cheese–filled pretzels in the shape of Mickey Mouse. Matt was a Disney expert—he'd been dozens of times since moving to Southern California—and I surprised myself by actually caring about the little bits of Disney trivia he was telling me, like pointing out the names of the stores on Main Street and explaining that a lot of them were the names of Imagineers who had worked on the original construction of Disneyland. Was I now a person who cared about Disney Imagineers? *I must really like this guy*, I thought.

When we got back to my apartment, we made out on my stoop for a few minutes. Then I turned to him and said, "So I know this is a little crazy, and normally I would *never* ask, but for some reason it feels totally normal to ask, so, um, do you want to come to dinner with my sister and her husband tomorrow night?" Karen and Steve were flying into town the next day, and we had plans to eat at an Italian restaurant in Venice.

He did. I went to bed that night, feeling giddy and excited, and wanting to talk to him on the phone until I fell asleep.

A COUPLE OF days later, I flew to New York for work. Matt drove me to the airport in my car and promised to take care of it for the week—he would move it on street-cleaning days and even take it to be washed. It felt like the most thoughtful thing anyone had ever done for me. Why had I come to expect that people wouldn't do nice things for me? Had I become too cynical, too quick to assume the worst of people? I was letting him do nice things for me, and so far, it hadn't backfired. He had the week off—the show he worked on had built-in "hiatus" weeks—and I semijokingly said that maybe he should come to New York with me. Even as I said the words, I was aware of my tone, a way of protecting myself from this grand gesture in case he said no. But I was ready to make the grand gesture.

He didn't seem freaked out by the suggestion, but on the plane, I wondered if I had made *too* much of a grand gesture. Who invites the guy they've been seeing for a week to come to New York with them? And what if he came, and it was a disaster? Then he'd be stuck in New York with me, and I'd have nowhere to escape.

When I got to New York, I had dinner with some of my friends, and Daniel said that I looked happier than he'd ever seen me.

"Well . . ." I said. "I met someone."

"Okay . . ." Daniel said. He'd seen my boyfriends come and go, and he also knew how dejected I'd been about my romantic prospects right before moving to L.A. "Say more."

"I just get a good feeling," I said. "Is it totally cliché to say he's not like other guys? But he's not. I swear. He's super into me and I really like him and, well, let me ask you—would it be insane if I got him a ticket to come to New York using my Delta frequent flier miles?"

Daniel laughed. "I mean, yes, it would be." He paused. "But you should *definitely* do it."

The next morning, I cashed in thousands of Delta miles. It felt a little reckless—I barely knew this guy, and now he was going to be coming to New York, on a ticket that I had bought, and staying with me while I went to work during the day—and was definitely not something I would have done even a year before. I would have been worried about what people would think of me if the trip went badly—*She knew him for like a week and then invited him to New York! Can you imagine?*—and also how the sting of rejection would have been heightened because I had taken this huge risk and it hadn't paid off. But I had to learn to trust my gut again—or maybe for the first time—and my gut was telling me not just that I wasn't going to get burned by this guy, but that he was worth it.

I thought about how I would never have offered to fly Luke to New York—I was way too concerned with playing it cool and trying to divine what he wanted and make myself into that person. With Matt, I had immediately realized I could be myself, and let myself do what *I* wanted, even if that meant something that would have previously scared the shit out of me.

I deserved someone who was excited about taking a spontaneous trip to New York to be with me. A couple of days later, Matt caught a flight to JFK. My sister and her husband happened to be in town from D.C. with their pug, and we met them in Madison Square Park. It felt easy and normal. We sat in the park and the dog climbed into Matt's lap. My sister snapped a picture. In the photo, we're laughing, our heads close to touching, around the dog. We look happy. We look like a couple.

"You guys are *cute* together," my sister whispered, as Matt and her husband talked about one of their shared interests—*Star Trek.* "He's so sweet!"

"Can you believe he came to New York with me?" I said. I still couldn't totally believe it myself.

"I can," she said, and I realized that one of the benefits of all the bullshit that had come before—the slow decline of my relationship with Jon, the anguish over Luke, all the not-horrible-but-definitely-not-great dates—was that I knew when something good had come along.

CHAPTER EIGHTEEN

The rest of the trip was the very definition of the honeymoon phase, in the best possible way: Matt walked around Manhattan visiting guitar stores and drinking coffee while I worked during the day, and at night I took him to my favorite restaurants and introduced him to some of my friends, and then we went back to the corporate apartment that BuzzFeed rented for its out-of-town employees and had sex. But even though it all felt so easy, there was still an undercurrent of anxiety. I wanted to just "be in the moment" and enjoy being with someone I really liked who seemed to really like me, but I also felt like I needed to hold just a tiny bit of myself back to protect myself. What if he turned out to be just another one of those guys who disappeared?

There was a part of me that was worried Matt was a "future-talker"—that is, someone who loved to talk about plans they had no intention of actually bringing to fruition. These are the guys who, on the second date, tell you that they really want to go on vacation with you, take you to a family reunion or to their company holiday party, or even just say that they want to go to a concert with you next month—but then they get squirrelly about scheduling anything for Friday night. I had gone out with more than a few of these guys and found that, at first, their enthusiasm was incredibly seductive— until I realized that they didn't have any intention of going on vacation or to the family reunion or the company holiday party with me.

The charitable explanation is that in the moment, these guys actually *do* believe they are going to want to go with you to whatever far-off event they have in mind. But its remove from reality means that they never have to follow through on their pie-in-the-sky plans, and they don't actually want to invest the time and energy one would need to get to a point in the relationship where it would be appropriate to take a partner to a family reunion. The not-so-charitable explanation is that these types of guys are possible sadists and revel in getting you excited about something that they know is never going to happen.

Before I met Matt, I had tried to unpack with Cynthia, my therapist, why I kept attracting future-talkers. "Is there something about them that feels comfortable or familiar to you?" she asked. "It's possible you're subconsciously replicating patterns that aren't necessarily healthy, but that are easy for you."

I thought about it. "Well, I guess my dad is kind of a future-talker," I said slowly. "I just remember him always talking about going on a trip or doing things that he never followed through on, but I'd get excited thinking they were going to happen. And, like, it was hard to plan stuff around him because he always wanted to 'keep his options open' about whether he might be traveling for business. Sometimes he would travel, but sometimes he wouldn't."

"We want our parents to be stabilizing, secure presences, so it can be disorienting when they're not," Cynthia said. "But you know—our parents are also human. They make mistakes, and a lot of the time they don't even know why they're making them."

I turned this over in my mind for a moment. "I guess I just ended up thinking that he was never going to follow through on *anything* he said he was going to do, because I didn't want to be disappointed."

"So it would make sense that you'd be attracted to men who come up with grand plans," she said. "It's a pattern that you're familiar with. And the disappointment is part of that pattern."

After things ended with Luke, it had occurred to me that there was something comfortable about his emotional unavailability. He wasn't a future-talker, but he remained forever somewhat aloof, out of touch. Future-talkers were kind of the other side of the same coin, but until now, I hadn't let myself fully unpack that, because what a cliché, right? *Woman has daddy issues and this leads to her fucked-up relationships with men.* This would also explain why I alternated between guys who seemed like the opposite of my dad in terms of being dependable and reliable, and those who seemed uncomfortably like my dad.

"Okay," I said. "So what if I want to break that pattern?"

"I think it starts with coming to terms with how you feel about your dad," she said. I realized that even if I never confronted him about it, I needed to forgive him—for my own sake. I had to deprogram myself if I was going to have any hope of making things work with Matt, because right now, I was so sure that he was going to disappoint me that I almost set myself up for it, and then I was surprised when he actually followed through on what he said he was going to do.

"Why is that surprising?" he asked me a couple of months after we started dating. "I said I would do something and I did it."

"I . . . don't know," I said. "I guess I'm just used to guys who don't follow through on things." He seemed genuinely befuddled by this, like it would not have ever occurred to him to say he was going to do something and then not do it.

I needed to give Matt the benefit of the doubt. Being a late bloomer may have meant that I recognized a good thing when I saw it, but it also meant that the memories of my past relationships were always lurking in the background.

A couple of months after we met, I turned thirty-seven. The morning of my birthday, we were at Matt's house, and he brought a wrapped gift to me. It was a framed print of an illustrated Harriet the Spy that he'd gotten on Etsy. She had her notebook, and big glasses, and her signature tomato sandwich, and a quote: "Is everybody a different person when they are with somebody else?" The print made me feel seen in a way that I'm not sure he even realized: For so long, I had contorted myself to be the person I thought guys wanted me to be, and I ended up just losing myself. Now, when I was actually being myself in a relationship, it turned out that the person I was with liked me more than ever.

BY THE END of the summer of 2014, Matt and I started casually talking about moving in together. It was too soon, we both agreed, especially since neither of our apartments was really suitable to house both of us, so we'd have to move into an entirely new place. January seemed realistic, we decided. And yet there could be no harm in just *looking* online to see what was available, right?

Matt quickly found something—a single family house not too far from where we both currently lived, a short bike ride from the studio where the show Matt wrote for, *@midnight*, was shot and similarly close to the BuzzFeed L.A. office. Three bedrooms, two bathrooms, parking. And it was relatively cheap, less than our combined rents. We should just go look at it, we decided. What was the harm in that?

I didn't love it. It had bland light brown carpeting in the bedrooms and the walls were painted a similar milky latte color—great for coffee, drab for halls. The living room was big and bright, but the kitchen was cramped and old, and the bedrooms were small. Surely we should keep looking, I told Matt, but he pointed out that there was nothing similar available in this neighborhood for the price, and it had a big yard and a patio, and the landlord agreed to provide washer and dryer hookups. Slowly, I was won over.

Buying a house was never on the table; neither of us had much in the way of savings, and real estate prices in Los Angeles were getting out of reach even if we had. The only people I knew who had been able to afford a house in L.A. had either bought it years ago or gotten help from their parents. We couldn't turn back time, and neither of our parents was in a position to help us. It seemed like the trade-off I had to make for living in L.A. was that some aspects of my life were just always going to seem suspended.

CHAPTER NINETEEN

"**I** *cannot* deal with her for one more second." The person sitting across from me was an editor, one of my direct reports, who oversaw the entertainment coverage on BuzzFeed. "She goes behind my back, her reporters cover the same thing our reporters cover and don't tell us, she complains about us . . . I just can't deal anymore," he repeated. The "her" in question was another editor in New York who managed celebrity news. They each reported to different people, in a managerial structure that made little sense except to protect certain fiefdoms at the company, and these two editors in particular were always at odds—and I was always in the middle of it. Ben, my boss, was impatient with the conflict and implored me to fix it. I would try, and then things would just go back to the way they were. It was infuriating, and petty. Couldn't everyone just relax and not be so territorial?

Apparently not. And generally, I was growing more and more disillusioned with work. Hadn't I been a creative person at one time in my life? It was getting difficult to remember. Now my days were spent in meetings and mediating disputes. I was wrestling with the fact that after two years, I still wasn't totally comfortable being a manager. I was never sure how much authority I was supposed to project, or how friendly I was supposed to be with the people who reported to me—and most of the editorial team in L.A. reported up to me. It created a distance that made being actual friends difficult. I was keenly aware of being "the boss," even though no one used that word. I could sense that there were definitely people in the office who just didn't like me, and I couldn't totally figure out why. Was it just because I was "the boss," or was there something I was doing that made me especially unlikeable? I wanted to be a person who didn't care that she was disliked, but it bothered me—and I didn't know how to fix it.

I saw other male managers who were friends with their direct reports, and I wondered whether it was something about being a man that made it easier to "bro down" with people who worked for them. That had certainly been the case at *Rolling Stone,* where it seemed like being a man conferred an instant insider status. But to a lesser extent that still felt true at BuzzFeed, especially when I'd been in the New York office. There was a group of guys who went out to lunch every single day, never inviting anyone else along; one of them ran a large editorial team, and he was best friends with a couple of guys who reported to him. Of course people are going to make friends at work, and it's unrealistic to expect that cliques won't form. It was just eye-opening to see how the same power structures that had felt inaccessible to me at *Rolling Stone* were so easily replicated at BuzzFeed.

Being a manager was not just exhausting, but also unrewarding. It was impossible to please everyone—something that made Ben happy would piss off someone who reported to me, or if I tried to stand up for my direct reports, I'd get shit from Ben. I was still under enormous pressure to have my teams not just keep their traffic up, but be part of "the conversation." Ben had a habit of sending terse emails late at night or very early in the morning, asking what was up with an article or, worse, one of my editors or writers. One of the ways that I found I could keep Ben placated was by responding almost immediately to his emails—he felt that people who didn't respond to him within minutes were blowing him off—and so I would scramble to respond to him whenever I saw his name in my inbox.

Once Ben had developed a negative opinion of someone, it was nearly impossible to change his mind, so I spent a lot of time trying to make sure he thought *I* was doing a good job, what is usually derogatorily referred to as "managing up." What I didn't realize until much later was that oftentimes, people who reported to me were *also* managing up, and I didn't always have a clear view of what was going on with their teams or whether people who reported to them were having problems, and for a long time I was too inexperienced as a manager to figure that out, to ask the right questions.

There's an assumption, in creative industries especially, that if you're good at your job as a writer or editor, then you'll be a good manager, but I can tell you that being an editor and being a manager are very different skill sets, and when it comes to the writers and editors I know, myself included, few of them are great managers. I started to wonder what it meant to be ambitious if the career path you assumed you'd be taking— and you assumed you would want—turned out to not be so appealing after all. I had never really articulated, to myself or anyone else, that I was "ambitious," but I felt like it was just implied. Everyone I knew wanted a promotion, to make more money, to get hired by the more prestigious website or magazine, and I had just gone along with that. But eventually, you had to stop, right? Very few people got to be editor in chief of anything. So if you weren't going to be an editor in chief, and you weren't going to try to get the job at the more prestigious place, where did that leave you? Were you just supposed to be *content* wherever you were? Was that just . . . giving up? Or— and this was a reframing that I had never stopped to think about—was it just an acknowledgment of what made you happy, and that was okay?

In the same way that I couldn't play the "cool" girl in dating any longer, I was growing disillusioned with following someone else's script for my professional life. I'd taken it as a given that being ambitious always meant getting the next promotion, and the next, and the next. But now I was asking myself, what if this wasn't something I really wanted—and if I didn't, did that mean I was a failure?

I NEEDED A writing project of my own, completely separate from anything I was doing at BuzzFeed—a creative outlet. A project that would just be for me, something I could lose myself in and not have to care about finishing performance reviews or responding to emails. I might not even let anyone else read it.

I decided the way to go about it was to write every day, no matter what, and keep track of the number of words I was writing. Isn't that what every famous writer ever always said, that the only trick to writing was to write every day? That way, even if what I wrote was total dreck, at least I'd be able, I thought optimistically, to be proud of writing thousands of words. It would be my New Year's resolution. I called it my January writing challenge.

I started by creating a character, a twentysomething guy living in New York named Nilay whose startup had just failed. The New York startup world was one I was pretty familiar with, both from working at BuzzFeed and writing about New York tech startups when I was freelancing. It was a funny little world, kind of a junior-varsity Silicon Valley, although of course no one there thought of themselves that way. I was particularly interested in the ways in which the New York tech scene was continually trying to establish legitimacy and power in a city that already had a lot of powerful industries.

I'd never written fiction before, except briefly in a short story class I took in college. I was a journalist, someone who observed the *real* world around her. But I found a certain liberation I wasn't expecting in writing fiction. Creating characters reminded me of the acting I did in high school, when I would have to embody a different person and try to understand their needs and wants and motivations. It was even more fun, I found, to actually make up these people myself and try to invent their needs, wants, and motivations.

I started to look forward to my morning writing sessions, especially to having something else to focus my thoughts on besides work. The house would be dark and quiet as I'd pad out to the kitchen in my slippers, make a cup of coffee, and take it into my office with me. I stretched out on the love seat in my office, my computer perched on my lap, and just let the words come as I sipped my coffee. I started thinking about what else could be going on with Nilay besides having a failed startup, and then I came up with another character named Katya, who was a reporter at a tech blog, and then I decided there should be another company founder whose company *was* successful, or at least seemed successful on paper, who was hooking up with a subordinate of his.

I kept track of the number of words I wrote each day on a spreadsheet. The numbers kept ticking up, and when the month was over, I had around forty pages of . . . something. Was it a novel? Was it something I should shove deep into my Documents folder and never speak of again? I wasn't sure.

My agent, Alia, had reached out to me a few years earlier after I'd written an essay for *Slate* about feeling like I was in a generation between Gen X and Millennials. I liked her right away—she was supersmart, no-nonsense, had good ideas, and seemed committed to developing my career long term. But we hadn't actually sold anything together yet. Now I emailed her and asked if she would mind reading something. "It's fiction," I wrote, "which I know is surprising, but it just sort of happened." I was nervous. What if she thought it was ridiculous that I had even attempted to write fiction? But she emailed me back right away that she would love to read it.

I prepared myself to hear that she didn't like it, and if that was the case, so be it; it had been a fun exercise, and it felt like an achievement to have written all those words either way. I realized that I had been able to put aside what other people might think and done something for myself, something that felt right in a way that my job didn't.

Alia got back to me a couple of days later. "I really like this," she said, "and I think you should keep going."

I had been so ready to hear that she didn't like it that I hadn't even let myself think about what I was going to do if she said she *did* like it. Of course I would keep going, but now I had to actually come up with a plot and see it through. And in a couple of months, I would turn thirty-eight. If I finished it, and it sold to a publisher, and it was published, I would be forty when it came out. Which didn't feel *old,* exactly, but the words *debut novelist* tend to conjure an image of a person in their twenties who just finished an MFA program, not a forty-year-old journalist. Even though I had told myself that I was writing this book for me, I still worried about conforming to the outside world's idea of what a debut novelist should look like. But even as I recognized that tension, I knew I had to move past it. My voice deserved to be heard as much as anyone's, whether I was forty or twenty-five. I was ready to take up space.

I recalled some advice I had given years ago to a friend who was contemplating starting an exercise program but was worried he was too old: *You're going to be thirty-four no matter what, so you might as well just do it.* That was how I felt about attempting to write a novel. Unless something horrible happened, I was going to be forty no matter what. I might as well turn forty having written a book.

Writing a novel reminded me of the time I spent training for the marathon. It was a long-term goal that I'd set for myself in large part to see if I could do it. And in the same way that in marathon training, three-mile runs turn into five-mile runs turn into ten- and fifteen-mile runs, the few hundred or so words that I managed to write each day gradually started to cohere into something resembling a narrative.

Then I got stuck. It was exciting to create these characters and to shape their inner lives and their moods and motivations, thinking about how they all interacted and writing scenes from my imagination. After around a hundred pages or so, though, I realized that what I had put together was essentially a series of scenes and character descriptions. The story itself was going in circles. I knew where I wanted it to end up, but I wasn't sure how to get there.

So I texted my friend Kate Spencer. Kate was a writer who I'd originally met through the internet—we'd both had Tumblrs in the early days of the site, when it was more of an old-school blogging platform than a home to memes and fan pages. A big theme of Kate's Tumblr was about coming to terms with her mom's death, and I'd found her writing to be simultaneously funny and poignant—a tough combination to pull off, but she managed it. We didn't meet in real life until years later, when we both had moved to Los Angeles from New York, not long after she'd given birth to her second child. I immediately liked her. Sometimes people have an online persona that's totally different from what they're like IRL, but Kate was the same hilarious, kind, thoughtful person I'd met on the internet so many years before. But she lived in the 'burbs and was busy with two small children, so we rarely saw each other.

But now, I wondered, maybe she would be interested in a writing group, made up of just the two of us? There were other people I was better friends with whom I could have approached, but I think I reached out precisely *because* we weren't super-close friends. I figured she'd be more likely to be honest with me about my work, and vice versa. She said yes, that she had been thinking about writing an essay collection centered around her mom's death and grief in general, and that she'd love to get my feedback on it. So we started meeting a couple of times a month, sharing work with each other beforehand and sending feedback.

Our two-person writing group was perfect. It was just the

amount of accountability I needed, but I also loved reading Kate's work, which—like her Tumblr—managed to balance being funny with real emotion, without veering into sentimentality.

A couple of months after we started meeting, I was at an impasse: Through no fault of Kate's feedback, the book had somehow ballooned into being told from a total of seven characters' perspectives—it was unwieldy and confusing, and the plot didn't totally make sense. I knew I still wanted to finish, but how? I worried that my book writing was going to end up being like my marathon training—I'd work really hard at it, and get superclose to the finish line, but ultimately wouldn't be able to complete it.

One afternoon, as Kate and I sat in a coffee shop near my house that was inexplicably reminiscent of the all-white decor in *A Clockwork Orange,* I told her I was struggling with plot and pacing. "I still feel like the middle of the book isn't there," I said. "It's too slow. I feel like not enough happens to move the story along, like I'm getting bogged down in description and characters."

"Hmm," she said. "Do you know what a beat sheet is?"

"You mean, like for screenplays?" A beat sheet is an outline of the "beats," or plot and emotional turns, of a movie. Most screenplays follow a very specific formula, even as the stories are different.

"Yes," she said. "I think it could be helpful. Just go back and try to write a beat sheet based on what you have, and then think about where you need to add plot."

I hadn't ever considered imposing this kind of structure on my work—it almost seemed like cheating. But there's a reason, I realized, that most movies follow the same three-act narrative structure. As audiences, we're used to it; it feels familiar, almost comforting to know that at the end of the second act, it will seem as though everything is going disastrously for the protagonist—the café she owns is going to fail, her boyfriend isn't speaking to her, her roommate has told her she's selling their house—when suddenly, she receives some new information and figures out a way to turn everything around! One of the restaurant's longtime patrons, the crotchety old man who sits in the corner and nurses the same cup of coffee all day, turns out to be a secret millionaire, and he's going to save the café, because the protagonist is the only one who's ever been nice to him! Her boyfriend realizes he was wrong, and her roommate is still selling the house, but now that the café is saved, she can afford her own apartment! The story then reaches its satisfying conclusion. Thinking about my book in these terms helped me realize where the pacing felt flabby and where I needed to put in more plot elements. I didn't need my book to be told from seven characters' perspectives—it made more sense to tell it from three. And I streamlined the story so that it wasn't veering off in a thousand different directions.

I also started reading page-turners—Liane Moriarty's *Big Little Lies* and *The Husband's Secret*, Paula Hawkins's *The Girl on the Train*, Jessica Knoll's *Luckiest Girl Alive*—and studying their techniques. I wasn't writing a mystery or thriller, but I wanted to understand how these authors managed to hook their readers and keep them interested. I knew that I was never going to write a serious work of literary fiction, the kind written by MFA graduates who win prestigious awards, because that's just not the kind of writer I am—although a part of me wanted to be that writer, to get the respect and the accolades that come with writing a book like that. Ultimately, though, I had to write the book I wanted to write and that I felt the best about, and I wanted to write a book that people devoured, that they couldn't put down.

I was worried that studying technique and using a beat sheet template would make me feel like a hack, but instead, it was freeing. Once I had a structure, I was able to be more creative, and eventually, Alia sold the book. I was going to be a debut novelist, three weeks before my fortieth birthday.

CHAPTER TWENTY

Matt and I got engaged in February 2015, a little less than a year after we met. We went ring shopping together, to an antique jeweler in Beverly Hills, and I selected a beautiful but understated Edwardian-era ring. Picking out the ring felt surreal. Ten months ago, I'd been grappling with the idea that I might be single for the rest of my life, or at least the foreseeable future. And now here I was, getting engaged.

The honeymoon phase of strolling around New York hand in hand may have been over, but there was still so much I loved about Matt. He was kind and generous, someone who always thought about other people before himself, and I loved that he was a nerd in a way that was wholly foreign to me— a true enthusiast, someone who had deep and abiding obsessions with things I had almost zero knowledge of: guitars, *Star Trek,* the Dave Matthews Band, comics, the Beatles.

It occurred to me that this was how he'd approached our relationship, too. It was like from the moment he met me, he had decided that he was going to be passionate about something new, and that something new was . . . *me.* In the past, someone being so into me might have freaked me out. I was wary of being put on a pedestal, but because I reciprocated Matt's affection it didn't feel weird.

No one seemed surprised that we'd gotten engaged so quickly. In my twenties and early thirties, people got engaged after being together for years; an engagement in less than a year was unheard of. But now, all I had to say was "when you know you know," and everyone nodded sagaciously—which confirmed, in its own way, that I *was* outside of the norm. I was more surprised that Matt, at thirty-one, didn't feel the need to wait. I thought about where I'd been at thirty-one: working at *The New York Observer,* living with Jon, and just starting to think about how maybe, one day, we would get engaged. I also thought about how different this felt than when I'd been with Jon, especially toward the end of our relationship, when I was despairing over his wishy-washiness. Jon had made me question myself. Matt made me feel secure.

LOOMING OVER OUR engagement like a fear-mongering women's magazine coverline was my biological clock. I had spent my twenties and early thirties ambivalent about whether I wanted to have kids. Matt was the first person I'd been with whom I could actually *envision* having children with—and the desire to have kids specifically *with him* manifested itself. And then, suddenly, I *really* wanted kids.

Even before I met Matt, though, I'd had an inkling that I might want to keep that option open. Nearly four years earlier, during the summer before I left New York, I had gone to the fertility clinic at NYU to get information about freezing my eggs. The doctor sat across the desk from me with a pen and piece of paper. "Here's how your fertility decreases in your thirties," he had said matter-of-factly. "Did you know that even with medical intervention, a woman your age only has a twenty percent chance of getting pregnant each month?" I gulped. This seemed to directly contradict everything I'd ever learned—or not learned—in sex ed. In high school, our teacher's version of sex ed consisted mainly of implying *very strongly* that all we girls had to do to get pregnant was approach a penis, like probably we just would have to be in the same room, but definitely, *definitely* if we were to ever get naked with a boy, pregnancy would be instantaneous, and it wouldn't matter if we were nowhere near our ovulation window: PREGNANCY WOULD HAPPEN. And then, of course, our lives would be over. (Also, since it was the nineties, every teenager I knew, myself included, was terrified of getting AIDS.) I think I knew on some level that this was a *slight* exaggeration, but there was zero instruction about ovulation or when in your cycle you can actually get pregnant, and I didn't bother fact-checking it myself.

So there I was, at thirty-five, sitting across from a wolfish doctor who seemed all too eager to get me to agree to pump my body full of hormones in order to have my eggs harvested. "You are born with all the eggs you will ever have," he said ominously. I imagined how many I had started out with and how many I had lost. The numbers seemed incomprehensible.

I didn't end up freezing my eggs—the combination of the cost (around $10,000) and stress made me second-guess my decision, and I also figured if I was going to need medical intervention to get pregnant, anyway, I might as well wait until I was more settled.

I'd also never been pregnant, so I had no idea if I could even *get* pregnant. I'd never even had a real pregnancy scare, just a couple of times when the condom broke and I got Plan B out of an abundance of caution, not because I was actually worried that I might get pregnant. Matt had also never gotten anyone pregnant, a fact that I noted and filed away.

A few months after we got engaged, right around when I turned thirty-eight, we had a conversation about starting to try to have a baby. I'd been off hormonal birth control for years, relying solely on condoms, and I read up on fertile windows and ovulation. I was a little older than was ideal, but there should, theoretically, not be an issue with getting pregnant.

"Do you think it's a bad idea to be pregnant at our wedding?" I asked Matt. "I mean, ideally, I would be out of my first trimester, because of nausea."

"Don't you want to be able to drink at your own wedding?" he said.

I shrugged. "I think I could still have, like, a glass of champagne. It just seems like given my age, every month counts, so I don't want to wait until after the wedding."

"Makes sense," he said. "Although it probably won't be as fun."

But it would be worth it.

CHAPTER TWENTY-ONE

I was not pregnant at our wedding, but a few of my friends, and my sister, Karen, were. I was excited for Karen's baby, her first; a few months earlier, my brother's wife, Alyson, had given birth to their first child. In my family, we did things in reverse order: My younger siblings had both gotten married and had kids before me. *We all do things on our own time,* I reminded myself.

But getting married last in my family also took some of the pressure off. My parents just seemed relieved that I was getting married, *period.* So they didn't protest when we told them the wedding would be in Las Vegas, or that Matt wasn't Jewish and we wouldn't be having a Jewish wedding. I was also one of the last of my friends to get married, and I had learned a lot from the weddings I had gone to. The most extravagant weddings were often not the most fun; my friends who had stressed the most about their weddings beforehand had been fixated on things that I just didn't care about, like the color of the napkins. Matt and I were in agreement: We just wanted to have a big party where our friends could get together, get a little tipsy, and dance a lot. (Also, we were paying for it ourselves, so we were trying to keep costs down.) The ceremony would be in a chapel at the Venetian Hotel; the reception would be on the large patio of one of the restaurants in the hotel; almost everything, including the decor, the flowers, and the food, were either predetermined or things we could pick from a small menu of options. I didn't want to be overwhelmed by choice or feel like I needed to throw the Best! Party! Ever! I was just happy to be marrying Matt.

I may have set my expectations kind of low, but our wedding was—objectively, of course—one of the best weddings I'd ever been to. People had *fun*. We didn't stop dancing. As a surprise, we'd hired an Elvis impersonator to show up halfway through the reception, and the crowd went wild for him. And the ceremony was so moving—we wrote our own vows, and I teared up as I was reading mine, and some of our guests cried too! I was just happy to be surrounded by so many people I loved, marrying the person I loved.

Then we left for our honeymoon to Reykjavík and London. After the high of the wedding, I thought, wouldn't it be just perfect if I got pregnant on our honeymoon? Wherever we went, the specter of the nonexistent pregnancy was always there. I tried to reassure myself by telling myself that it had only been a few months, and we'd been "trying" before the wedding but not *really* trying, not like obsessively charting basal temperatures to know when I was ovulating or making sure we had sex multiple times during the so-called fertile window. We hadn't been treating trying to get pregnant like it was our job. But when we got back, I thought, we could *really* start trying.

I had friends who had run the gamut of infertility experiences—miscarriages, IVF, struggles to get pregnant—

but I also knew people who had gotten pregnant immediately, even well into their thirties. My friend Bridget told me I shouldn't worry that I was too old to get pregnant easily. "You just have to have sex the day *before* you ovulate," she said one night when we met for dinner. She was around my age and had a two-year-old. "I did that and we got pregnant *right* away. You'll be fine."

I got ovulation strips that would supposedly tell me the ideal moment to have sex. "I usually tell people to go to a reproductive endocrinologist after a year of trying, but at your age, you can go after six months," my doctor said, when I asked her when we should start thinking about intervention.

Matt was convinced the problem lay with him. "I think it's my weight," he said matter-of-factly. He had lost weight in the months before I met him, but now was starting to gain weight again: "My balls probably get so hot, with all that extra weight." I laughed. That couldn't be true, could it? There were plenty of fat people, men and women, who managed to reproduce.

"I doubt it's you," I said. "It's probably me, and my old eggs."

IN JANUARY 2016, Karen had her baby, a girl. I happened to be in New York at the time and took the train down to Washington, D.C., to meet my new niece. D.C. had been walloped with a snowstorm that weekend, and when I got off the train at Union Station, the city seemed eerily quiet. There weren't any cabs waiting in front of the station, so I decided to walk to their house, which wasn't far. As I walked down the mostly unshoveled sidewalks, I thought, for the millionth time, about how my younger sister had managed to achieve so many life milestones way before me. Karen had always been much more type A than me, certainly, but she also had a nearly unshakable sense of self and thus has always been able to fulfill the promise and potential of the person she knew she was. She knew she wanted to be a lawyer from the time she was in high school and went straight to law school, and now, at thirty-one, she had her first child, a job as an associate in a corporate law firm, the top two floors of a townhouse in a charming neighborhood in D.C. I knew that I shouldn't compare myself to her—although we were very close, we were also very different people. Her friends mostly worked in finance or law and had followed similarly straightforward tracks to the comfortable upper-middle-class lifestyle they aspired to. Still, it was hard to look at her life and not ponder the existential questions, like whether *I should have gone to law school* and *maybe I *should* have married my college ex-boyfriend.* I knew deep down that I didn't want her life, but from the outside at least, it seemed so appealingly uncomplicated and fulfilling. Why did I insist on making things harder for myself?

My sister—who normally had everything hypertogether—looked exhausted. "The hospital was a shit show," she said, sitting on the couch in their living room as she attempted to nurse the baby. "And we were trying to get out ahead of the blizzard, so everything was rushed and I got to the car and realized they had forgotten to take out my IV."

"Shut up," I said.

"Swear to god," she said, rolling her eyes. "And I didn't even notice because I was just so frantic trying to get out of there."

"Ugh," I said. "I'm sorry."

Karen put away her boob. "Do you want to hold her?" she

asked, holding the baby out to me. I took her from her hands and rocked her in my arms. She was tiny and soft. *You didn't exist outside of my sister a week ago,* I thought. It was an obvious, banal observation, but somehow, seeing my niece here, in the literal flesh, was making me more emotional than I had expected.

I stayed a couple more days and then took the train back to New York, and on the flight back to Los Angeles, I got my period.

CHAPTER TWENTY-TWO

I probably should have started calling doctors right away, but I waited until the last day of April, when it was almost exactly six months from when I'd seen my OB, and called someone I found by looking in *Los Angeles Magazine*'s Best Doctors issue. She was in her sixties, very no-nonsense. She told me my uterus looked good, but to make sure, she sent me to get an exam during which your uterine cavity gets filled with an X-ray dye, to see if your fallopian tubes are clear and if anything else abnormal shows up in your uterus. At the same time, she sent Matt to get a semen analysis.

My tubes were clear, but a polyp had come up on the exam, and I'd need to get it removed before I could potentially start fertility treatments. Meanwhile, Matt had gotten the results of his semen analysis, and they were not good, just as he had suspected. I hated that he had been right about this, but the doctor downplayed the notion that he had a low sperm count because of his weight. "We just don't know why," the doctor said. "It could be any number of things." Our official diagnosis was male factor infertility, and my doctor said that we would have a less than 1 percent chance of conceiving without medical intervention. All those months of dutifully checking ovulation strips and having scheduled sex had been pointless.

I started an accordion file with our test results and diagnoses, and notes from the doctors. I was ready. I would be the General Patton of infertility: organized, efficient, ruthless. Infertility had no idea what it was in for.

I quickly learned that infertility laughs in the face of plans. Every step of the way, it seemed like there were roadblocks. My ob-gyn didn't do polyp removal surgery, so I'd have to find someone else. I finally found a surgeon who would do the operation using my insurance, and the morning of the surgery, Matt and I took a selfie as I waited in the pre-op bed. This would just be something to check off the list, and then I would be able to start IVF treatments and then I would get pregnant and we would have a baby—right? I didn't want to let myself think about what would happen if it didn't work. I was finding that the more complications that came up, the more I wanted it to work, and the more it seemed incredible that people had babies without medical intervention. Imagine, just having sex and getting pregnant! It seemed so easy, and so cheap, and so unfair that it wasn't accessible to us.

Still, it was hard to actually picture what motherhood would be like. It seemed so far off in the distance. I had so many hurdles I had to overcome before I held a baby in my arms that I felt like I needed to just focus on the here and now: Get this blood test, have this surgery, meet this doctor. Picturing a future that might not exist for me was too overwhelming, but I could schedule an ultrasound. That was something that was still in my control.

Soon, we met our new doctor, who came recommended by one of Matt's friends. Matt had been much more open about our struggles getting pregnant than I was. He told me he'd brought it up at his weekly poker game and was surprised to learn that three other people at the table were either currently undergoing treatments with their partners or had done fertility treatments. He talked about it on the podcasts he recorded, joking about his "dumb sperm."

I was more circumspect. I told some close friends, but I hadn't written about it online or on social media. I didn't want to admit it to myself, but I felt like a failure just by virtue of having to do infertility treatments, even if they were ostensibly because of Matt's "dumb sperm." All the times I had felt like I hadn't gotten the memo about some unwritten "girl code"— whether it was about shaving my legs or trying to not date a guy I worked with who lived with his girlfriend—seemed like they had now converged on my fertility. Maybe my ovaries hadn't gotten the memo either.

And I wondered if we'd be in the same position if I *had* frozen my eggs. Then I wouldn't have to go through the egg retrieval now, three years later. I had thought doing an egg retrieval at thirty-five would be the same as doing IVF at thirty-nine, but they weren't the same at all.

Our doctor was a tall, thin, bald man who wore glasses. Matt disliked him immediately. "He didn't laugh at my jokes," he said when we got home from our first appointment with him. "He's a robot."

"God forbid someone doesn't laugh at your jokes," I said. I didn't find the new doctor particularly warm, but he seemed careful, methodical. "We need a doctor, not an audience for your jokes."

. . .

TO PREPARE FOR the egg retrieval, I had to inject myself for ten or so days with a cocktail of fertility meds to help my follicles develop. The meds made me nervous. They were expensive—we had no insurance coverage for them, either—and they required me to be exacting, injecting at the same time every evening with a specific, and often changing, amount of drugs. I worried that I would spill them or inject myself with the incorrect dose. At each ultrasound appointment, my doctor seemed pleased by the progress of my follicles, and as the scheduled day for the retrieval approached, I was cautiously optimistic. Matt seemed optimistic, not even cautiously.

"I think we'll get four embryos," Matt said.

"How will we choose which one to transfer?" I asked. "If we get four embryos, what will we do with the extra ones?"

"I don't know," he said. "I guess we'll figure it out."

On the third day after the retrieval, after all the eggs had been fertilized and were growing in the lab, we got an update that there were nine embryos that were still growing, but by day five, there were only four. Then the four were biopsied, and we waited for the genetic testing results that would tell us if the embryos we'd created were viable. We finally got the results: Just one embryo was genetically normal.

I couldn't believe it. How had we gone from nine embryos on day three to one normal embryo? It seemed mathematically perplexing, but that was infertility math—like the hardest, most ruthless math you've ever encountered. My doctor didn't have any real explanation, just telling us that there's no way to predict how many normal embryos you're going to end up with, and there's always a large drop-off between the number of eggs you get and the number of normal embryos you get.

Finding out the biological sex of the embryo from just a few cells is truly a weird experience. I'd asked the clinic to withhold the sex, but when they had emailed us with the results of our genetic tests they had referred to the embryo as female. Of course, what I was afraid of happening, happened: I started thinking about a little baby girl, one who would have dark hair like Matt and me. She'd be smart, funny, kind, and hopefully not as moody as I had been as a teenager (but I'd definitely get her on antidepressants if she needed them). Matt's vision of our daughter was a funny tomboy. "You know that means she'll be super into, like, princess stuff," I told him, but he shrugged. We'd come up with a list of names—Matt was pushing for Regina or Gloria, after his grandmothers; I liked Alice, or maybe a name like Estelle or Annette, something that sounded like it could have belonged to one of my grandmother Jeannette's friends.

WE DID ANOTHER retrieval that summer, and that yielded us one normal embryo and one "inconclusive" embryo. I got an email from the clinic's embryologist that read, "A segmental error was reported on the second embryo, indicating that part of one arm of chromosome 2 in the biopsied cells from that embryo was deleted. Chromosome numbers were normal, but a chromosome segment was partially misrepresented . . . Our industry is still trying to define which of the segmental errors are of clinical significance. Some may self-correct, and some may not translate to errors in the fetus (which is a good possibility with this particular deletion). In short, based on the current genetics literature we can speculate, but cannot ascertain with certainty, which errors might be associated with abnormalities in offspring."

In other words: They had no fucking idea. All I wanted were concrete answers, and it was becoming increasingly clear that when it came to fertility treatments, there were no concrete answers. There often weren't any answers, *period.*

As the summer wore on, I started noticing that more and more people were responding to Matt on social media about going through fertility treatments. I was getting more frustrated—that it wasn't working, but also that our health insurance didn't cover any of it. I tweeted about my frustration, and to my surprise, the responses were sympathetic and kind. I started wondering if *I* should be talking about what we were going through more openly. I had been nervous about being more public about our struggles, but now that I had, I was relieved. And I felt a sense of kinship and community with everyone who tweeted back at me. They *got* it.

But I was also sensing a shift in myself, in how I was starting to feel about doing IVF. It may not have been working yet, but by talking about it publicly, maybe I was giving myself space to be who I really was.

I suggested to Matt that maybe we continue talking about doing IVF—on a podcast. Together. In real time.

"No one wants to listen to us talk about IVF," he said.

"I think they do," I told him. "Look at all the guys responding to you on Twitter about how they're so glad you're talking about it."

"I guess there aren't a lot of men who talk about infertility," he said. "I don't care, I'll talk about my dumb sperm all day."

"There aren't a lot of women who talk about it openly, either," I said. "It's got such a stigma attached to it." I paused. Did it really, though, or was it a stigma that *I* had attached to it? I wondered, Would doing a podcast together help me work through some of my own insecurities around doing IVF? "I really think we should do a podcast. Why don't you do a Twitter poll and see if people want us to do one?"

"Fine," he said. "There's no way that they're going to say they want one."

But people did. The official results of the poll were 80 percent in favor, 20 percent opposed—more in favor than I had even anticipated. We launched *Matt and Doree's Eggcellent Adventure* in October 2016, a few weeks before my first embryo transfer.

"We're not sure how long this podcast is going to last," I said on the first episode. "Maybe it'll be a limited series. Like six episodes."

It seemed like a reasonable number.

CHAPTER TWENTY-THREE

The prep for an embryo transfer is similar to the prep for an egg retrieval, with one significant difference: You inject your shots in your butt. Well, not exactly your butt, but just above your butt, like the back-butt region. The needles for this injection were scarily long and the angle for the shot required some creative contortion. Matt ended up doing most of them, but as the day of the transfer approached, he asked if it would be okay if he went to Las Vegas with his friend. I said okay, even though I was a little annoyed that he would even ask. *I* couldn't just up and go to Las Vegas; it was yet another example of the ways in which this whole process affected the two of us so differently.

That night, I twisted around and tried to find the exact angle that I was supposed to be injecting—it would be really bad to hit a muscle—took a deep breath, and plunged it in. It definitely did *not* go in correctly. When I took it out, the needle was bent at a ninety-degree angle. "*Fuck,*" I said. I'd probably failed to inject the correct amount, and as an added bonus, my ass was now on fire.

I called Matt, crying. "I just tried to inject myself and I bent the needle, and I don't know if I got the progesterone in, and WHY AREN'T YOU HERE!" I'd once thought that I could approach IVF like General Patton, but maybe I was actually more like Napoleon, cocky and overconfident, only to suffer ignominious defeat at my Waterloo, aka my bathroom. And right when I needed Matt the most, he was probably sitting at an Iron Man slot machine, losing money that we would need for our inevitable next round of IVF.

"I'll come home," he said.

"You don't have to do that," I said, sniffling.

"No, I'm coming home," he said. "I shouldn't have gone anyway."

The transfer itself was relatively straightforward. There was no anesthesia; I just got wheeled into the OR and lay there, watching on a monitor as the doctor inserted a catheter into my vagina and deposited the embryo, and then he handed me a printout of the embryo. And then came the wait, an agonizing ten days where I had to continue doing the progesterone shots to support the embryo that may or may not have implanted. It seemed like it had to work—why *wouldn't* it work? It was a genetically normal embryo and there didn't seem to be any other issues.

The problem with progesterone shots—besides being completely impossible to do yourself—is that they mimic the early symptoms of pregnancy. So my breasts were tender; I felt tired and moody. In the new *Matt and Doree's Eggcellent Adventure* Facebook group, people warned me not to "symptom spot"—that is, not to assume that any twinge of symptoms I felt definitely meant that I was pregnant. But it was hard not to, even though I knew it could just be the progesterone talking.

On day ten, when I went into the clinic to get the blood test that would tell me if I was pregnant, I felt cautiously optimistic. I hadn't taken a home pregnancy test, because I was worried that whatever the result was would make me anxious.

"Good luck," the phlebotomist said as my blood dripped into the test tube.*

My nurse, Lila, called while I was having lunch with my friend Alie. I went outside to take the call. "I'm so sorry, Doree," she said when I answered the phone. Lila was a beautiful Iranian woman who had a stapler in the shape of a black stiletto high heel shoe on her desk. "You can stop all your medications now." She told me that my HCG level was zero, meaning the embryo had completely failed to implant at all.

There wasn't going to be a Regina or Gloria or Alice or Estelle or Annette. When I got home from lunch, I tore up the picture of the embryo and threw it in the trash.

---

* Another unexpected and unwelcome result of doing infertility treatments: Someone is *constantly* taking your blood. When you're getting monitored in the days leading up to your egg retrieval, you have to go into the clinic multiple times, and each time they take at least two vials of blood. Which wouldn't be such a big deal if I wasn't what the phlebotomists rather grimly call a "hard stick," meaning that my veins are tiny, deep, and difficult to find. They "roll," which is not a good thing. It usually took two to three tries for the phlebotomist to access them, and so by the end of a retrieval cycle, my arms were so bruised it looked like I'd been beaten up. Finally, I learned to ask for the one guy who could always get my vein on the first try. If you're like me and you have shitty veins, FIND THE GOOD PHLEBOTOMIST.

. . .

A COUPLE OF MONTHS later, I was back at the clinic, and my doctor had an ultrasound wand inserted into my vagina as I lay back on an exam table. Matt sat in the corner, eyes on the monitor that would show the contents of my ovaries. We were hoping to do another egg retrieval right away.

"Hmm," my doctor said. "You only have a couple of follicles on the left, and one on the right. I don't think we should do a retrieval this cycle." Ideally, at my age, I would have had five to ten on each side.

"What?" I said. "Does this mean I'm just . . . done? Like this is the number of follicles I can now expect?"

"No," he said. "It can vary from month to month. Are you under a lot of stress?"

I couldn't help myself—I laughed. "I mean, of course I am, this whole situation is very stressful!"

"Well, you should try to be less stressed," the doctor said.

"Like . . . how? Should I do acupuncture?"

He shrugged. "I mean, you *could.*" He seemed uncomfortable. "All right, well . . ." he said, and left the exam room.

That night, I told Matt I wanted to switch doctors. "I told you when we met him that he was a robot!" Matt said.

"Okay," I said, "you were right. Happy?" Matt loved to remind me when he had been right about something, and most of the time, I didn't want to hear it. I wanted to be comforted and told everything would be okay—not a smug "I told you so."

But despite the stress I was under, I knew I was one of the lucky ones, because even if we couldn't *really* afford to be doing all these rounds of IVF, we had a lot of credit cards and I was

THANKS FOR WAITING 181

getting very good at the zero percent balance transfer game, and there are many, *many* people who can't afford fertility treatments, period. That said, I was kind of kicking the can down the road in terms of paying off the cards. We had *just* finished paying off our wedding when we started infertility treatments. It seemed impossible that we would ever be out of debt or that we would ever be able to own a house. I checked Zillow obsessively just to "get a sense of the market," and the sense of the market I was getting was that anything that would have remotely been within our financial reach in Los Angeles was quickly snapped up, and prices were increasing at an alarming rate.

Also, Matt and I didn't see eye to eye on buying a house. "Why would we tie up cash and take on even *more* debt that we wouldn't pay off for thirty years?" he asked. "And if we own a house, we'd be responsible for everything that went wrong. It would be expensive. And there's no guarantee that we'd make back the money we put into it."

I tried to explain the concept of "building equity" and it was like I was speaking a different language. He listened skeptically, then said, " 'Building equity' is just not something that's important to me. I like to have liquidity." He said he couldn't see himself as a person who would spend the amount of money that you needed to spend to get a house in Los Angeles.

"We could have liquidity, *and* a safety net, *and* build equity," I said. "I mean, not right now, because we're tens of thousands of dollars in debt, but one day."

"Sure," he said, in a tone that said he was pretty confident it was never going to happen.

"It's not just about the money, though," I said. "It's about making a home and having a place that's *ours*. A place for our family. Putting down roots." My dad may have traveled a lot, but we lived in the same house from the time I was in kindergarten, and I liked that feeling of being home. It was familiar and comforting. I wanted to have that again.

But I didn't have to add that our family might always only consist of the two of us.

CHAPTER TWENTY-FOUR

In the midst of the various rounds of fertility treatments, I had started going to a barre class on Sunday mornings. Barre is a workout that's heavily marketed to women that involves doing lots of planks, very small movements of various muscles with one- to three-pound weights or a rubber ball, and an extended segment of class at the ballet barre, where you do a lot of leg exercises that may lead you to wonder whether barre class should be permitted under the Geneva Convention. The classes promise a variety of questionable benefits, mostly involving making your ass higher and tighter. Short of butt implants,* there is pretty much no way that my ass is ever going to be described as anything besides "just this side of flat," and that's being generous.

---

* You can tell yourself that you're just voyeuristically browsing online plastic surgery forums where women show off their new Kardashian-inspired butts only so many times before you start wondering, *Wait, do I want a Brazilian butt lift? Is the recovery really that bad? Could I finally wear a pair of jeans without looking like my body was just a pair of legs somehow attached to a torso?*

Anyway. My presence at this particular class had been inconsistent. It had been hard to become a regular while doing IVF treatments, because the treatments have the unique ability to fuck up your life in unpredictable and highly annoying ways. IVF is your shitty ex who never wanted to make plans more than half an hour in advance, and when you've finally moved on, sends a "u up?" text and next thing you know you're at their apartment making out on the couch. They both wreak havoc with your emotions, make it impossible to plan, and drag you back into their orbit against your will.

I had stopped going to barre in the weeks before my second egg retrieval, because the hormones that I had to take to stimulate egg production also made my ovaries huge and tender, so I couldn't work out after day five or so of doing the meds, or else I ran the risk of my ovaries contorting or bursting. I had been warned that this would be the case going in, and because I was prepared, I was mostly fine. Whenever I know what's coming, I'm able to wrap my head around it, but living in any kind of uncertainty is hell. I'd like to pretend that I'm one of those people who can just roll with it, but when the plan changes halfway through, I get agitated in a way that makes me feel like a child whose mom promised them ice cream but then the ice cream shop is closed, and they have to get candy instead, and the candy is *fine* but the kid is like, *Mom, why did you promise me ice cream when I can't even get ice cream, and now I want ice cream even more.* Like I know I'm wrong, but the world seems wrong, too.

In a way, it brought back uncomfortable reminders of online dating, when I struggled so much to be the "easygoing" and "flexible" woman that I thought guys wanted, or as way too many online dating profiles put it, "I want a girl who's just as comfortable going out in heels as they are staying in and wearing sweatpants." We're told we need to simultaneously be quote-unquote high maintenance, with everything that goes along with that characterization, and also "chill," "down for whatever."

No wonder I struggled with this for so long—the person society told me I should be wasn't truly the person I was, and pretending to be that person gets exhausting. I was never *actually* cool with it when someone canceled plans at the last minute, or a guy didn't text back. It really fucking bothered me! But I spent a lot of time just acting like it didn't, because that was how I thought people wanted me to be.

And being "chill" about infertility just . . . doesn't work. Postretrieval, I had really been looking forward to getting back to my workout routine, and specifically, to my Sunday morning barre class. But infertility threw another wrench in my plans: It turns out that you can't work out until you get your first period postretrieval, which totaled around three to four weeks of not being able to work out, and as someone who wasn't in perfect shape but used exercise to help support her mental health—this was a problem. I couldn't even do a gentle yoga class, because you're always just one seated spinal twist from ovarian contortion.

Finally, the Sunday after I had gotten my period, I was cleared to go back, and I was *psyched.* What I had put out of my mind was that so many of the other women (it was always women) in the class were in extremely good shape. At this particular class, I immediately noticed an extremely thin and muscular woman with a long, thick blond braid down her back and a crop top that showed off her six-pack. She stood at the front of the room scowling in the mirror, and when the class started, I saw that she was using extra weights for all the exercises. *Deep breaths,* I thought. *In Los Angeles, there are many, many people whose actual job it is to be attractive.* And just when you think you've conquered any lingering insecurities about your body, someone comes along who's like, *Bwa ha ha, you can pretend all you want that this shit doesn't matter but GUESS WHAT, IT DOES, and I am going to make you feel bad about yourself!*

The woman in barre class not only made me feel bad about myself, but she also looked angry and mean, like she had moved to L.A. thinking she was going to be the next Jennifer Lawrence but hadn't landed any roles more interesting than "white party girl #2" on her friend's web series. That's another thing about L.A. Someone can be the prettiest girl in their high school class, or the star of all the musicals, or maybe even be in a local car dealership commercial, and then they come here and they realize that sure, they're still pretty and talented, but it's not enough, and then they end up in a barre class looking like they want to kill someone.

In that sense, there's freedom in being "average" looking— I never had any illusions that I would need to rely on my looks for anything. But we're all just at the mercy of the patriarchy, right? When I say that I'm completely average looking, by what metric am I even judging that? A metric that, for millennia, has been determined by men, internalized by women, and spat back out in the form of color-blocked leggings and matching sports bras.

I kept an eye on her the whole class. She attacked the exercises with grim determination, using the heaviest weights in the class and squatting lower than anyone else. I was, quite honestly, in awe. I lingered for a moment in front of the mirror after class ended as she carefully gathered her things, and I was suddenly overcome with the urge to cry, right there in barre class. We'd been doing fertility treatments for a year, with nothing to show for it but a ton of debt and a frozen embryo that might or might not turn into a baby. Friends, many of whom were younger than me, were having their second or even third children, or had kids who were in grade school or beyond. They were selling their first homes and buying bigger houses in nicer neighborhoods. And there I was, in barre class, obsessing over a woman with a perfect body and wondering what the hell I was doing with my life.

CHAPTER TWENTY-FIVE

A couple of months before my novel *Startup* came out in April 2017, I got drinks with my friend Amanda from work. Amanda is ten years younger than me and an incredibly smart reporter. "So," she said, as we sipped our drinks, "how do you feel about your book coming out?"

"I feel okay," I said. "I mean, I feel good. I just don't know what to expect."

"It will be great," Amanda said.

"I hope so," I said. "I just want to be able to call myself a novelist. Does that make sense? Like, when do I get to call myself 'a novelist'?"

Amanda looked confused. "Um, right now? You *are* a novelist! You wrote a novel!"

She was right, of course, but it was hard for me to wrap my head around. Even though my book was being published by a major publisher, even though it had already gotten positive early reviews, I still felt like an interloper in the fiction world. Who was *I* to think that I could just swoop in and write a novel? But no, I had to remind myself, I had worked really

hard on the book. And my book *was* good. I *could* call myself
a novelist.

It struck me that I was still struggling, at nearly forty years
old, with the same issues I'd had for so long: Where did I belong in the world, and what contributions was I going to make
to it?

When the book was published, I was pleasantly surprised
by the good reviews and positive reception that it received.
The night of the release, I did a reading and conversation at
Housing Works, a bookstore in Manhattan, and the place was
packed—standing room only. Some people were sitting on the
floor. People I hadn't seen in years were there. I was emotional—
all those people were there *for me*! Back in L.A., after a reading
at Skylight Books, we had a small party at a bar nearby, a kind
of combination book party and fortieth birthday celebration.
Matt got a cake for me in the shape of my book, and everyone
toasted me, and it felt good.

But turning forty was a real maelstrom of mixed emotions.
Hanging over everything was the fact that I still wasn't pregnant.
And even though my book launch had been a success, I was still
struggling with questions of identity. Not being pregnant made
me feel broken, like I sucked at doing this really basic thing that
literally billions of people have done for centuries.

And my internal struggles were spilling out into how I pre-
sented myself to the world. It turned out I had no idea how to
dress myself anymore. For most of my thirties, I'd had a work
uniform: floral or patterned silk top, skinny jeans, ankle boots.
Sometimes I'd invert it and do patterned pants with a solid
color top; there had been some slight variation with button-
down plaid shirts and skinny jeans when I was at *Rolling Stone*

because I was, consciously or not, trying to fit in with the guys who worked there. But now, when I put on skinny jeans and a top, it didn't feel like *me* anymore. The jeans weren't especially comfortable, and in the morning I scanned my closet in increasing desperation as I eliminated each shirt, one after the other, from daily contention.

I was also having trouble shopping, which had historically been a pastime that I truly enjoyed, perhaps a little too much. But now, when I went into my old standby stores—shops like Madewell and Topshop and Club Monaco and Zara and H&M—I was having an increasingly hard time finding clothes that appealed to me, and actually fit. My turning forty also coincided with the truly unfortunate fashion trend of one-shoulder or shoulder-cutout tops, a look that was very difficult to pull off without a strapless bra, and I'm sorry, but if you're above a D cup, there is no strapless bra on the planet that will be comfortable for you. (If there is, please send one to me.) I could have worn one of these shirts or dresses with my sensible beige Maidenform racerback bra showing, but that seemed to negate the whole point of these tops in the first place. Not wearing a bra wasn't an option; it's a matter of physical comfort. It's *achy* to have them just flopping out there in the wind (and don't even get me started on boob sweat).

I had never been someone who felt like I needed to "dress my age," and yet now, all of a sudden, I was willing to dress my age but I had no idea what that even looked like. What were forty-year-old women even supposed to look like?

I HAVE, for better and (for my own mental health) for worse, always been someone who cares about how I look, and how other people think I look (see also: Revenge Jacket Doree). And I have also always been a faithful student of the people around me and what they were wearing, like a little proto-Harriet, always watching and absorbing.

When I was four, a girl in my class at daycare had a pair of yellow clogs that I wanted so badly. I begged my mother for them and she (wisely) said no, that I was only four and I would probably break my ankle.* So I didn't get the clogs, but I did get extremely concerned with having cool clothes and shoes. This really picked up speed in third or fourth grade, when I finally persuaded my mom to buy me a Benetton rugby shirt, which seemed to be the absolute pinnacle of cool at the time. Don't forget, it was the eighties, and some diabolical genius had convinced us all that rugby shirts with huge logos on them looked amazing. "It's literally just a shirt with a big brand name on it," my mom said, and I nodded enthusiastically. Wasn't that the whole point, to show everyone you could be part of the club by wearing a really dumb-looking shirt with a truly massive logo on it?

By seventh grade, I could buy my own clothes because I had my own money thanks to babysitting, because at the time, eleven or twelve was a perfectly reasonable age to watch other people's children for money.† This meant I had enough money

---

* Fast-forward almost forty years, and I've almost broken my ankle approximately one million times in my years wearing clogs. I don't want to say Mom is always right, but she was right about clogs and ankles. That has not stopped me from buying many pairs, however. You can't stop me now, Mom!!!!

† Of course, this now seems insane. These days, if people saw or heard about an eleven-year-old babysitting, the police would probably arrest the parents who hired the babysitter *and* the babysitter's parents. But in

to go to the juniors department at Filene's in the Chestnut Hill Mall in Chestnut Hill, Massachusetts, aka the *fancy* mall that had a Laura Ashley store and a Houlihan's, and buy, for sixty dollars, a pair of tight, acid-washed Guess jeans with the triangle Guess logo on one of the back pockets. This seemed like the most money that anyone had ever paid for a pair of jeans, and I counted out the cash slowly and proudly and wore those jeans with my Nike Airs and my teased bangs until, all of a sudden, it was the nineties and "tight" and "acid-washed" and "teased bangs" and "pegging your jeans" were no longer part of the teenage fashion lexicon. Instead it was all about going to the Urban Outfitters on Newbury Street or Harvard Square and wearing flannels and Doc Martens and vintage overalls and "streetwear" brands like Stüssy and Fresh Jive. Probably because I lived in Massachusetts, I'd had an intermediate stop in preppy land—J.Crew rollneck sweaters, moccasins from L.L.Bean, a CB jacket with ski lift tags hanging on the zipper all winter, you get the idea, it was all sort of tragic—in between the phases of looking like I'd walked off the set of a John Hughes movie and onto the set of a Nirvana music video.

Being a teenager sometimes feels like you're the costume designer for the movie of your own life (but of course, actual

---

seventh grade, I had a regular job watching two brothers a couple of days a week after school, where I mostly spent the afternoons playing Tetris on their home computer after heating up some SpaghettiOs for the boys. More shockingly, I also had a regular gig with a three-month-old whose parents finally stopped calling me once she started crawling and somehow broke the glass door of their stereo cabinet, at which point they probably realized that there had rarely been a better example of getting what you pay for than paying an eleven-year-old six dollars an hour to watch an actual infant.

movies like *Clueless* and *Kids,* which both came out the summer after I graduated from high school, were hugely influen-
tial too). Every time I decided to start dressing a different way,
it required an almost entirely new wardrobe, although there
was occasionally some overlap: For example, I'd procured a few
flannels when I was in my preppy phase, which transitioned
seamlessly into grunge.

But one of my biggest fashion influences during that time
was my friend Beth, whom I'd met the summer after my senior
year of high school when we both worked at a restaurant on
Newbury Street in Boston. Beth was a year older than me, a
photographer and film student at NYU, and she was *cool.* She
was living for the summer in an apartment in Cambridge with
her older brother—again, *cool,* seeing as I was stuck at home—
and as soon as we got off work, we'd traipse down Newbury
Street, sitting on the floor of Tower Records and reading magazines for hours, sipping coffee at Espresso Royale, trying on
clothes and shoes at Allston Beat. She wore drain chains for
necklaces and babydoll tees and baggy pants, but also slips as
dresses and turquoise nail polish. One night, I met her at her
brother's apartment, and we went out in Harvard Square. I had
carefully considered my outfit for our excursion, which deliberately channeled Garbage front woman Shirley Manson, if
she had shopped in the bargain bin at Urban Outfitters: a
zebra-print velour miniskirt, a short-sleeve black polyester col-
lared shirt that looked vintage but wasn't, fishnets, black John
Fluevog boots, and a red patent-leather spiked bracelet.

It was a Look. Of course, "looks" are different when you're
eighteen and using them as armor, to try on an identity you're
not quite ready for. But now I was forty, and I was, once again,
tentatively dipping a toe into a new identity, except this time

it was wearing a sensible low-heel shoe with a nice wide toe box. I had naïvely thought that, as I aged, I'd be able to continue operating in the same way that I had been since I was a teenager: There constantly would be a plethora of trends and looks for me to choose from, and all I had to do was select one.

And while on the one hand I resented the idea that I should "dress my age," I also really just wanted to . . . dress my age. I didn't want to wear anything tight or see-through or too short; I wanted to feel comfortable, but not like I had totally abandoned all pretense of caring about how I looked, because I do care about how I look and I don't want to pretend that I don't. But all around me, all I saw were clothes that I couldn't imagine putting on my body.

"Is this where I admit that I now understand the appeal of a store like Chico's?" I asked Kate. "Like, all I want to do is dress like a funky art teacher. I never wanted to look like this before."

"Yes. I get it. I now understand the appeal of purely comfortable clothes," she said.

"What is *happening* to us?" I said, laughing. "I guess I just never thought this would happen to me."

Then, one day, I was in a shop near my house and I spotted a sleeveless, oversized, black linen jumpsuit. I tried it on. It was looser than almost anything else I owned, but instead of feeling like a blob, I felt airy and free. It exposed my upper arms, which I had historically kept covered because . . . why? I suddenly wasn't sure. I thought about how all my body insecurities—my "flabby" upper arms, my "paunchy" stomach, my "too thin" legs, my "too thick" waist, my "flat" butt, my "big" boobs—had dictated what I wore and, perhaps more significantly, what I didn't wear. It seemed exhausting, this automatic fixation on "flattering" clothes and covering parts of my body up that didn't need to be.

I bought it. It became my nonwork go-to, the item of clothing I wore most often. It felt both slightly childish and, somehow, with its lovely drape, sophisticated. I felt more like myself than I had in ages.

CHAPTER TWENTY-SIX

The seasons of infertility are marked by whatever appointments and procedures and results you've gotten. There's the Spring of Initial Optimism and Polyp Removal, the Summer of Disappointing Retrieval Results, the Fall of the Failed Embryo Transfer. I was hopeful that the summer of 2017 would be the Summer When Things Finally Started to Go Right.

I had a new doctor, Kelly Baek, and I immediately felt more comfortable with her. She was obsessed with getting results for her patients, but she also was straightforward. When we first met with her, she told me she was concerned about the first embryo transfer, the one that had failed. "Your HCG was zero," she said, referring to the hormone that's present when you're pregnant, "which means that the embryo didn't implant at all." She said she wanted to do an endometrial function test, which would determine if the embryo had been transferred at the optimal time for my uterus, and she would also check my uterus for any abnormalities. To do the test, I would have to take all the meds that I would typically take for a transfer cycle, but they'd just do a biopsy instead of a transfer at the end of it.

I grumbled about it on our way home. "It's just another

dumb roadblock," I said to Matt. "They're not going to find anything, and in the meantime, we're set back another month or two from doing a transfer." A month here, a month there—it didn't seem like much, but before I knew it, another year had gone by.

A FEW WEEKS LATER, I was in a tiny exam room at my fertility clinic getting a microscopic camera inserted into my vagina. It hurt. I lay back on the exam table as the doctor—not Dr. Baek, who had injured her knee and couldn't physically do the exam I needed—cracked jokes and told me about growing up in Brooklyn and being a fan of the Mets. "See that? Now we're getting to your uterus—" He stopped talking and immediately the joviality was replaced by a grave look. "Get Dr. Baek," he said to the nurse in the room. "*Immediately.*"

"Um . . . is everything okay?" Even as I asked, I knew it wasn't, but the way the mood in the room had changed so quickly was jarring and I hadn't quite caught up.

He shook his head. "No. It's not," he said as Dr. Baek came hobbling into the room. The other doctor pointed to the image of my uterus on the screen. "See that?" he said to her. She nodded grimly and put her hand on my arm. "You have a uterine septum," he said. "When you were born, the two sides of your uterus never fused, and so an embryo can't get the blood supply that it needs when it's transferred. That's why your transfer didn't work."

"Oh," I said. My head was spinning. "How did this happen?"

"We don't know," Dr. Baek said. "It's something you were born with. Only three percent of women have them. The good news is, it's easily fixed with surgery." I would need to have a surgical hysteroscopy to repair my septum and fix my uterus. Then I would have to wait another couple of months before we could do a transfer, to let my uterus heal.

I walked to the car, slightly dazed. It was a lot to process at once. Three percent! Why couldn't I be on the winning side of 3 percent, like one of the tiny percentage of women who gets pregnant without IVF after being told they need to do IVF? *That embryo never had a chance,* I thought bitterly. *If only they had done this before they transferred it, they would have known about it, and maybe it would've worked.* I didn't want to think too much about it.

More jarring was the realization that in fact, there *had* been something wrong with me this whole time.

NOW THAT WE were doing the podcast, and I was public about doing IVF treatments, everyone wanted to talk to me about infertility. I usually didn't mind, but sometimes I did.

At work one day, one of my colleagues cornered me. "My wife's cousin had been trying for *years,*" he said. "And then, right when they were about to do IVF—like, their appointment was *the next day*—they found out she was pregnant. How crazy is that?"

"So crazy!" I said, even though what I really wanted to say was, *Please leave, this story is only going to upset me and it's even more upsetting that you somehow think you are doing me a favor by telling it to me.*

"I know, I couldn't believe it!" he said. His face was eager, as though waiting for my acknowledgment that *his* story would be the one that would make me realize that this, too, could happen to me, if I just, I don't know, heard enough stories about miracle babies?

By that point, I had heard all the stories. And they always started the same way, with a well-meaning person who, upon hearing that I was doing IVF, simultaneously expressed sympathy but also brightened a bit. They had something they couldn't wait to share, something that would *definitely* make me feel better about the hellish road I was on.

It would turn out that their friend's roommate's cousin's sister-in-law—or, wait, was it the best friend of someone they went to college with? Or maybe it was their partner's co-worker's ex-wife. Yes. That's who it was, definitely! Anyway, this person, whoever she was, had been doing IVF for years and, whaddya know, spontaneously got pregnant with a "miracle" baby, just when they had given up hope and stopped trying. Or *wait*. Was it that they were *about* to do IVF and got pregnant with a miracle baby? No. Sorry. It was when they went to *Aruba* as a consolation for IVF not working that they got pregnant—because they had stopped trying, of course. And then there was the person who already had two IVF babies and wasn't on birth control because the doctors had said they had a .00000001 percent chance of getting pregnant on their own, and then it happened, as though the pregnancy goddesses are sick fucks who will only allow pregnancy to occur once you've given up or completely stopped trying. (The implication is related to the "advice" given to single people that "once you stop looking, s/he will appear!," which I personally also think is bullshit because meeting someone, especially over the age of thirty-five, is actually hard work.) These

are the same people who earnestly suggest that you try meditation and acupuncture, as though you weren't already meditat-
ing and acupuncturing like it was your job, and as though
they—random person who has never themselves undergone
infertility treatment—have the solution that you and your doctors have somehow never heard of. "But look, they *totally*
helped my friend's sister," this person will say, just as you want
to smack them.

In my head, whenever I would hear a story like this, I
would make a long fart sound, but in real life, I forced a smile
as the person babbled on and on with their cheerful miracle
baby story. On the podcast with Matt, I was emphatic in my
distaste for these "miracle baby" stories. "Who are these stories
helping?" I asked. "They're not meant to make *me* feel better.
They're totally self-serving. People just want to feel like they
can feel better in the face of something they can't fix or control." What these people didn't know is that anyone going
through infertility has *long* since reconciled themselves with
the idea that most of what they're going through is out of their
control. In these moments, all I could think is that the things
I would most like to control were the words coming out of this
other person's mouth, and preferably to shove them back in.

Matt was horrified that I would be so "rude." "These people are just trying to help," he said. "They're just trying to *relate*
to you."

"I know," I said. "And I'm saying that it doesn't work, and
it's not helpful. I know their intentions are good, but maybe
good intentions aren't good enough, okay? And I'm also allowed to find what they're saying to be *really* fucking annoying."

"Okay," Matt said. "You *are* allowed to do that."

. . .

AS SOON AS my body had healed from the septum resection-ing, we decided to do another embryo transfer. For the trans-fer itself, I had to have a full bladder, because Dr. Baek said that a full bladder helped her guide the embryo in (in contrast to my previous doctor, who wanted an empty bladder). A nurse did an ultrasound to check my bladder when I got to the clinic. "Not full enough!" she said cheerfully. "You've got to drink more, dear."

As I lay on the pre-op bed, guzzling water, I tried to stay calm. Another nurse came by and offered me a Valium. "You don't have to take it, but it might help you relax," she said. I took it.

Finally, it was time to go into the operating room. Matt sat next to me, holding my hand. I lay back, my feet in stirrups, as we looked up on a screen where an image of the embryo was on display. Dr. Baek confirmed with the embryologist that it was the correct embryo, and then it was loaded into a catheter that she inserted into my vagina, navigating past my cervix, and finally inserting it into my uterus. "That's it," she said. "All done."

In a way, it was anticlimactic, but maybe that was the Va-lium talking. After the last transfer, with its complete lack of implantation, I didn't want to get my hopes up, but it was al-most impossible not to. Isn't optimism ultimately part of the human condition? If we didn't have optimism, why would we have persevered over millennia of hardship, if not for the faith that things would one day get better? My uterus was fixed now, the embryo had been genetically tested. According to my doctor, there was a 70 percent chance that it would work.

Those were good odds, but like everything else when it comes to IVF, numbers can sometimes feel meaningless. What was I supposed to do with the knowledge, for example, that only 3 percent of women have a uterine septum? The odds were overwhelmingly against my having one, and yet, I did. So even as I told myself that this time, the odds were in my favor, I was also worried that once again they would not be.

THE PREVIOUS SUMMER, right around the time we started IVF, we'd gotten a dog—an eighty-pound goofball rescue pup named Beau who was either one and a half or three years old, depending on who you asked. And soon after we adopted Beau, the lease on my convertible was up, and when we went to the dealership, we had decided to get the largest SUV that Volvo made, because it didn't seem crazy to think that by the following summer, we'd be driving a dog and a baby around. The massive SUV would be able to carry us all, with room to spare for a stroller, a diaper bag, and whatever other gear tiny humans needed carted around with them.

But the car took up too much space—physically and mentally. When I got behind the wheel, I felt like a suburban mom, except that there was no one in the back seat. As the months went by and I didn't get pregnant, it became an expensive reminder of the life I thought I'd be living by now, but that remained stubbornly, frustratingly out of reach. Whenever I would have these thoughts, I would remind myself that I was fortunate to be in a position where I could afford a large SUV and where I could afford to be doing IVF, and then I would feel guilty about being upset that the car had become an albatross and that I should, in the immortal words of Rihanna, just shut up and drive.

I googled "can I get someone to take over my car lease." The short answer: probably. The car was, actually, way too big for me. I not so jokingly called it the boat, but it really felt like I was piloting a blimp through the streets of Los Angeles. If I'd had trouble driving my previous car, I now felt like I had lost all sense of peripheral vision. "You don't know how big the car is!" Matt would say, the exasperation clear in his voice, as I'd pull into the driveway with yet another scrape or scratch. One day, I obliviously took a piece of the fence on the edge of our driveway with me as I pulled into my parking spot, which I only learned when Matt got home and said, "Did you *not notice that you took a piece of the fence with you?*"

The day after the embryo transfer, I picked up my sister, brother-in-law, and niece from the airport. We decided to stop for lunch on our way home at an outdoor shopping center in Culver City. I dropped them off and drove into the multistory parking structure. It was lunchtime, and the lot was packed. As I drove up the ramps to the upper levels, I started worrying that there weren't going to be any more parking spots, and I'd have to drive out and find my sister and her family, and then I saw a spot next to a column. I turned in extra carefully, so as not to hit the expensive car to my right, and heard the telltale *CRRRRRUUUUUNNNNNCCHHHHH SCRRRRREEEEECH* as I scraped the driver's side of my car against the concrete column.

"Fuck. Me," I said to no one.

I carefully opened the door to inspect the damage. "Oh fuck," I said again. The rear driver's-side door and the quarter panel behind it were completely gouged. I had been extremely lucky not to have hit the shiny orange sports car next to me. Just like when I had driven into the side of the garage at my old apartment, the only damage was to my own car.

TWO WEEKS LATER, I found out that my HCG level was six; a pregnancy is usually anything over fifty. It was most likely a chemical pregnancy, or what should more accurately be called a tease pregnancy, a phantom pregnancy, a pregnancy that allows you to glimpse, for the briefest of moments, a future where you needed a car that fit a dog and a baby and a stroller. For days, I obsessively googled message board posts, trying to find anyone who had had such a low first HCG reading and had gone on to have a successful pregnancy. It wasn't impossible, according to my doctor, but very unlikely. Still, I held out hope. Maybe this time, the smallest odds would actually be in my favor.

CHAPTER TWENTY-SEVEN

When I think back on the brief period working in the internet 1.0 boom, I always think about how so many companies that flamed out spectacularly were just ahead of their time—like Kozmo.com, which, if you don't remember, was an online delivery service that would bring you pints of Ben & Jerry's within an hour. They opened up in 1998 and were shut down for good by 2001—ten years before Postmates. It was a good reminder that being first doesn't always mean you win.

I also think about how, at one company I worked for, everyone was granted stock options, and at a company-wide meeting one of the co-founders confidently told us that the company was worth $70 million. (It wasn't. Not even close.) Soon after I left for grad school, the stock market tanked and the same company had to lay people off. Then 9/11 happened, and most of my friends in New York lost their jobs. Things got better, and then they got bad again—*really* bad—which was when I lost my job at the *Observer.* And now some of the same things that had contributed to the first internet boom and bust were happening again. Companies, especially digital media companies, had taken on too much venture capital, with the assumption the exponential growth they'd been experiencing would last forever. Even I, who took a grand total of one college-level econ class, can tell you that exponential growth never lasts forever. In the years since I started at BuzzFeed, they'd taken on an astronomical $500 million in additional venture capital funding, but by the fall of 2017, revenue was falling short, and the company announced it would be laying off around a hundred people.

Almost immediately I got several panicked messages over Slack—the workplace instant messaging app we used to communicate with one another—from younger colleagues who were shocked that this had happened at BuzzFeed. They'd been in high school or just starting college when the Great Recession hit in 2008; they'd only ever worked for a company that was a total media darling, where new people were hired every week, where there was frozen yogurt on demand and free lunch multiple times per week. In contrast, I was always waiting for the other shoe to drop, just like all the other elderly (that is, anyone over thirty-five) people on staff.

I tried to be less "horribly jaded old lady" and more "supportive and wise elder" in my responses. "I know it's hard to see people being let go," I typed. I wanted to tell them that we'd been lucky that we hadn't been hit by layoffs already, but I figured that probably wouldn't help.

"Do you think there will be more?" one of them asked.

"I think your job is safe for now," I wrote back, not really answering the question. I should have been more straightforward, but I couldn't bring myself to tell them that there's truly no such thing as a free lunch, even when it's Taco Tuesday at work.

It was a grim time, and a grim reminder that capitalism

is ruthless. Don't be fooled by a company that tells you that everyone who works there is "like a family," because it's usually just something they say to get you to work longer hours and never see your actual family, until the day they lay you off, which they will do without a second thought, and all the free BuzzFeed knit hats in the world won't make up for a shitty severance package and having to pay for your own health insurance.

I didn't get laid off that day, but I was struggling at work. After a particularly rough period where it became clear that I couldn't successfully manage editors in New York from my post in L.A., I successfully navigated a transition from editor and manager to senior writer, first for the Culture desk and then for the Tech desk. The stories I wrote were generally well-received, but I'd been feeling increasingly despondent about my job in the last few weeks; after a couple of big stories over the summer, I hadn't written anything particularly groundbreaking lately, and I started getting obsessed with the idea that I was going to get fired. No one had indicated to me that this was the case, but because I wasn't writing as much as I thought I should be, I was feeling like a problem child—an *expensive* problem child, because I was still making the same amount of money that I had been making when I was an editor and manager.

"If you want to quit, you should quit," Matt said. "We'll figure it out."

"I can't just quit," I said. "I mean, right? I have this job that people would kill for. Jobs like mine are not that common in journalism right now. I can write pretty much whatever I want, my editors are great, I like my colleagues . . . fuck, what's wrong with me?"

"Maybe you've just outgrown it," he said. "It's okay."

"I guess I just feel guilty about quitting a quote-unquote dream job," I said. But in actuality, the BuzzFeed job had never been *quite* what I wanted—or what I felt like I was good at. Then again, what job *had* been fulfilling? The *Observer,* for a while. Gawker, occasionally. *Rolling Stone*—no. I suddenly realized, with a terrifying clarity, that the media jobs I'd had had all, in their own ways, made me anxious, made me second-guess myself, made me feel like nothing I did was ever *quite* good enough.

"Well, set that aside," Matt said. "If it's not *your* dream job anymore, then it's not a dream job."

EVEN THOUGH MY HCG had risen for a week after the initial reading of six, it still seemed unlikely that I was actually pregnant, but I had to go see my doctor for an ultrasound to make sure. "I'm sorry," she said, as she tilted the monitor toward me so I could see what she was pointing to. "You have a sac, but it's empty." I nodded mutely. "Why don't you get dressed, and then I'll come back and we can talk about it."

When she returned a few minutes later, I had a question. "I don't understand why my HCG was rising, if there was nothing in there," I told her. Even after all this time undergoing fertility treatments, when nothing ever made sense, I was still looking for an explanation.

"I know," Dr. Baek said. "The embryo was really trying to make it."

That was when my eyes welled up, as I thought about this embryo that was struggling to stay alive. Even though I knew on a rational level that I was assigning agency to a collection of cells so small it was barely perceptible to the naked eye, I felt protective of its struggle and fate. I also didn't understand it. Why had I undergone the septum surgery, all the prep, the retrievals, only to be confronted with yet another failure? It just didn't seem fair.

There was another layer to my sadness: the knowledge that Matt and I would have to discuss it on our podcast that weekend. In the year since we'd started doing the show, an incredible community had sprung up around it. There was a Facebook group with thousands of members who loved having a safe space where they could talk freely and privately about their fertility struggles without being judged, and where no one was allowed to use cheesy infertility message board terms like "baby dust" or "frosties" (baby dust is what you "sprinkle" to have good luck in your attempts to get pregnant, and "frosties" are frozen embryos). And we got dozens of emails each week from listeners who wanted to share their experiences with infertility or ask us for advice. By sharing our experience, people had felt emboldened to be more public about their own.

Of course, we didn't *have* to be so open about every single detail of the IVF process; it was our podcast, and technically we could talk about anything we wanted to. But we'd brought our listeners along on every doctor's appointment, every procedure, every blood test. It felt unfair to not tell them what had happened. I also knew that our listeners, more than anyone else, would be able to empathize with and understand what I was going through, because so many of them had been down the same road.

But sometimes, I regretted doing a podcast about our fertility treatments in real time. Because IVF hadn't worked, was I letting down our listeners? Did they see us as "characters" in an ongoing infertility saga, and was I disappointing them by not giving them the storybook ending they craved? I *wanted* to be able to give them that storybook ending, because it was the ending that I wanted for myself. "We can try again," Dr. Baek said. "When you're ready." I nodded. I was so sick of coming to the clinic. I had just assumed I would follow a story arc that went something like, protagonist visits fertility clinic, protagonist gets pregnant, protagonist has baby, protagonist is triumphant and lives happily ever after. Instead, my story felt more like I was trapped in the movie *Groundhog Day*, but set in a fertility clinic, which sounds like possibly the worst movie ever made.

But *why* had I expected that the story of trying to get pregnant would follow some predetermined arc? I'd already had to learn that my path—whether that meant career, marriage, or financial stability—was more meandering than I might have thought it would be. But I'd never before felt like I had so little control over the outcome. Until now, it wasn't like everything had worked out perfectly for me, but when things didn't go the way I wanted them to or had expected them to, I could course correct. I was ashamed that I had never really considered what it meant to always have options, even if they weren't necessarily the options I wanted; it was a privilege, I realized, that had gone pretty much unexamined until now. And maybe, I thought, this was a part of growing up that I still needed to do.

PART THREE

CHAPTER TWENTY-EIGHT

Do you want to start a podcast about skin care?" The text was from Kate, my friend with whom I'd been in a two-person writing group when I'd been working on *Startup*.

It was the fall of 2017. Donald Trump had been president for most of the year, and people seemed to be looking for comfort wherever they could find it. Skin care suddenly felt like a necessary coping mechanism. It was something I could control, in a world where so much was out of my control—a feeling that, thanks in large part to infertility, was all too familiar. Self-care was taking on new meanings as I navigated this new world of external and internal challenges. Instead of looking to the beauty industry to impose its often toxic standards on me, or the almost-as-nefarious "wellness" industry, with its juice cleanses and similarly unattainable and unhealthy body ideals, I was looking for something I could dictate the terms of. It was time to reclaim what it meant to care about what I looked like, how I saw myself, how I wanted to be seen by the world.

It seemed I wasn't alone. Kate and I had been texting about skin care for the past few months, and on social media, women

I knew who I'd never before seen discussing beauty products were suddenly fixated on the ideal shade of red lipstick or which serum would make their skin perfectly smooth. For the first time, it felt like we were participating in beauty culture not for status or for the benefit of the male gaze, but for ourselves.

I especially needed all the creams and serums, because as a BuzzFeed News reporter, I wasn't allowed to protest, call my reps, knock on doors, or donate money. Journalists were supposed to be "objective," which meant never publicly taking a position on anything political. I had chafed against this restriction before, but now, having to pretend to be "objective" felt particularly out of step with the moment we were in. In January, I went to the Women's March in downtown Los Angeles, carefully removing the BuzzFeed patch from my backpack and not posting about it on social media. I hated feeling like I had to hide my beliefs in the service of some nebulous, arbitrary notion of objectivity, and thus I had retreated into self-care and comfort, while simultaneously trying to write stories for BuzzFeed that put forth a progressive point of view without being explicitly "political." It was a tricky needle to thread, and one that I was growing increasingly resentful of having to thread in the first place.

So the text from Kate, coming at a moment when I was feeling especially impotent, seemed like a respite, an escape, a manifestation of a desire that I hadn't even known I was subconsciously putting out into the universe. I don't know if she was actually expecting me to say yes, but I responded immediately: "YES. YES I DO."

. . .

I WAS ENERGIZED by my new project. It was a welcome distraction from work, which I was feeling more and more hopeless about, and IVF, which I was trying and failing not to feel hopeless about. I'd learned enough in the year that we'd been doing *Eggcellent Adventure* that I was confident that Kate and I could produce the new podcast pretty easily with some outside help, and so we hired a producer named Samee to come on board. The show would be roughly an hour long, we decided, with some discussion between us at the beginning of the show, an interview, and some "intention setting" at the end of each episode; each week, Kate and I would come up with something we intended to do the following week. Our intentions could be anything that felt like they were broadly in the service of self-care—drink more water, fold the laundry, meditate for five minutes a day, call a friend. We agreed that our guests had to be racially and ethnically diverse, but we decided to try to only have female or nonbinary guests on the show, as a kind of antidote to the overwhelming maleness of the podcast industry.

From the start, it felt right. I loved working with Kate— she was smart and funny, and we were on the same page about pretty much everything. We weren't beauty influencers or even amateur makeup obsessives; we were just two women approaching middle age who wanted to unpack our place in the world and be in a conversation with each other and our listeners. And we could do *whatever we wanted to.* I remembered the moment when, writing *Startup,* I realized I had the power to make my characters say or do anything. No, I could do this in real life. There was no corporate overlord telling us we had to mention a certain product because they were advertising that week or interview a vapid but popular celebrity because it would get listeners. We could interview the people we wanted to interview, talk about the things that we wanted to talk about. As we geared up to launch, I felt professionally fulfilled in a way I hadn't in ages. All this time, I'd been chasing a dream in journalism, and I'd gotten the dream job, only to realize that it wasn't a dream job *for me*. The podcast felt like the thing I was finally meant to be doing.

Kate and I may have agreed on almost everything, but we couldn't agree on a name. I suggested *Women of a Certain Age*, which we liked but didn't love, and then my friend Jane Marie, who ran her own podcast studio called Little Everywhere, suggested *Forever35*—a kind of play on the fast-fashion clothing store Forever 21 that would make light of the period of life at which many women felt like they started to become invisible. We were here to make those women—and ourselves—more visible.

When we started the show, Kate was thirty-eight and I was forty, and we decided we wanted to target women around our age, who felt like they had been left behind by most fashion and beauty media. There's a peculiar but profound deflation in clicking on a story about someone's "minimalist" skin care routine and seeing a fresh-faced twenty-five-year-old who not only doesn't even have a zit, but also has nary a wrinkle on her smooth, glowy skin. Please come talk to me about your minimalist approach when you're forty-four and still getting pimples and your skin is dry and you have wrinkles and dark circles and are those new freckles? Nope, they're age spots, and no hundred-dollar cruelty-free all-natural face cream is going to help.

The goal with getting into skin care was never to seem ageless, or even just younger than I actually was, but simply to look in the mirror and be content with what I saw there, which had always been a challenge. As a teenager, I had moderately bad acne—or at least, it seemed bad at the time. Now I wonder if it truly *was* that bad, or if all those nights when my mom would position me under the reading lights above her bed to pop my pimples made me think that my skin was worse than it actually was. A dermatologist prescribed me Retin-A, which dried out my skin and made it peel off, and I was also on the swim team, which dried out my skin even more. As an adult, I was still addicted to popping my pimples and overanalyzing every blemish on my face; I spent way too many years staring at my skin in the mirror and not liking what I saw. Now, at forty, I had an opportunity to reframe the narrative I'd always told myself about my skin and my appearance, and I would do it publicly. If that made people uncomfortable, so be it.

WE RECORDED THE first episode in Kate's converted garage office space. "Hey, welcome to *Forever35*, a podcast about the things we do to take care of ourselves," Kate said to kick things off. "I'm Kate Spencer."

"And I'm Doree Shafrir," I said.

"And we're not experts, we're just two friends who love to talk about serums," Kate said.

After much discussion, this was the tagline we'd landed on that we felt perfectly reflected who we were and what the podcast was. Just a few years ago, I would have scoffed at the idea of doing a podcast about self-care. Taking care of myself was something that I never consciously thought about. I was too wrapped up in worrying what other people thought about me to look inward and care about myself. But now, I didn't even mind that the term *self-care* had itself become a ubiquitous chimera, at once everywhere but always just out of reach. There was a Goop-y version of self-care, one that said you could only be taking care of yourself if you spent a lot of money and had access to exclusive things, like $400 facials and $75 candles. Instead, our version of self-care—which posited that paying off your student loans was just as much self-care as the ideal night cream—felt more down-to-earth and accessible. And along those lines, we wanted to make it clear that we weren't approaching beauty and skin care topics from an expert point of view—we'd never been beauty editors or worked at women's magazines; we weren't even skin care "influencers." We were just two women aging out of marketers' target demographic who needed an outlet to discuss whether eye creams were a scam, and we wanted to let our listeners know that it was okay for them to discuss these topics, too.

It seemed appropriate to have Jane Marie on as our first guest—she had coined the podcast's name, after all—and we recorded the episode, our second, at her studio. As we sat around the table, the conversation flowed. Jane was funny. We were good at this! Kate had never hosted a podcast before, but she was a natural.

The podcast was a success in a way we hadn't really anticipated. We thought our conversations would strike a chord with women our age, but we hadn't realized how many women like us had felt that they weren't really being seen—by the media, by their friends, by their partners. Suddenly we were inundated with emails and voicemails from women grateful to be listening in on our conversations. They asked us for advice not just about night creams and serums and lip gloss, but also about whether they should break up with their boyfriends and girlfriends, how to deal with a mean boss, what to do when all your friends were pregnant and you weren't, how to find a therapist. They wanted to know which books they should read and which TV shows they should watch. They told us we felt like their big sisters and their best friends.

We were thrilled with how the podcast had so quickly found an audience, of course, but it was also a bit overwhelming. On top of my job at BuzzFeed, Kate and I were prepping the shows, booking the guests, editing the episodes (our producer, Samee, did the actual editing, but we sent notes), and of course, recording the episodes, which we were doing at night, usually in Kate's converted garage office space. It was a lot of work, but I was invigorated in a way I hadn't been in years. Even before the show had launched, we had signed our first advertiser, a website that helped people book vacation homes. I'd never sold ads before, but I sort of knew how they worked thanks to *Eggcellent Adventure,* and I decided that I could wing it, at least at first—and it would save us the commission that an ad network would charge us.

"I think you'll be able to quit your job soon," Matt said one day.

"No way," I said. The podcast still felt like a side hustle to me. If we brought in some extra cash because of it, great, but it didn't feel like it could be our full-time jobs.

"I think you'll be making your BuzzFeed salary by August," he maintained.

I wanted to believe him, and I desperately wanted to quit my job, but I was scared to be leaving a job that offered (relative) stability and health insurance, and even more scared to be doing it at forty. I had a feeling that if I left BuzzFeed, I might never have a full-time job again, at least not in media. I thought about all those meetings I'd been in over the years. There were never any women in their forties and fifties, just dudes. It seemed like just another way that older women were put out to pasture—certainly taking a hiatus from full-time work might not be the best idea from a career standpoint. And I knew countless freelancers who would have killed for a staff position, which are increasingly fewer and farther between. It seemed foolhardy to just give it up. I also needed to admit to myself that I had been holding on to the BuzzFeed job in part because of the promise of twenty weeks of paid maternity leave—a benefit that I wouldn't get if I were freelancing. But I'd already put the car before the baby, as it were. And with no pregnancy in sight, it was starting to seem quixotic to hang on to the job any longer than I needed to. In fact, staying at BuzzFeed to get paid maternity leave was starting to just throw the fact that I *wasn't* pregnant into even greater and sharper relief.

At the same time that *Forever35* was taking off, my job at BuzzFeed became even more challenging. I worked for a few weeks on a profile of the diversity officer at a startup in San Francisco, but when I sat down to write the story, it felt trite and superficial. I turned in a draft to my editor, who responded that she thought it needed a lot of work, and as I tried to revise it, I felt the motivation leaching out of my body. I realized that despite the stability that my job offered, I didn't want to be doing this anymore. I didn't want to be working for someone else, making money for someone else, following someone else's rules about what I could and couldn't say on social media or where I donated money.

I was also keenly aware that if I had been forty and single, without the support and financial safety net of a partner—and the ability to get on Matt's health insurance—I probably wouldn't be able to quit, or at least, it would have been a lot harder. It felt so unfair that so many self-help books just breezily advise you to take that leap of faith! Quit your job! Start your company! The rest of your life starts NOW! The truth is, so many of the people who are able to do that are *already* in positions of privilege. I wasn't blind to the privileges that I had that allowed me to even consider taking that leap of faith, to be a rat in a maze and finally see the way out.

STILL, I WAS scared shitless when, just a few months shy of my forty-first birthday in 2018, I called my editor, Ellen, to tell her I was leaving. I liked Ellen a lot—she was a great editor, supersmart, and around ten years younger than me.

"You know . . . I had a feeling you might say that," she said.

"Really?" I said.

"I was going to talk to you about it at your review," she said. *Oh right,* I thought—I was supposed to have my review the following week. So, in other words, I'd just made Ellen's life easier because she didn't have to have an awkward conversation with me about whether I really wanted this job, which as everyone knows is just code for your manager trying to get you to quit so they don't have to fire you.

When I told Ben, he seemed surprised that I was leaving for a podcast. "Huh," he said, in the way he said "huh" when he didn't really understand why you were doing what you were doing. "Well, I'm going to miss you," he said.

"I'll miss you, too," I said, and I meant it, but I also *wasn't* going to miss BuzzFeed, or working for Ben, because it was time to move on.

The last time I'd left a job without something else lined up had been when I was laid off from the *Observer*, and now that it was done, I started to question my decision. What if the podcast didn't work out? What if, after a few months, I *wasn't* making any money and I had to start looking for a new job and now suddenly I was old and out of the loop, and no one was returning my calls? *Then* what? I'd been turning around these "what if" scenarios in my mind so many times that I worried they'd become a self-fulfilling prophecy.

But instead of seeing it as a leap into the big, deep, scary unknown, I needed to see it as taking charge of my own career destiny. After six years at BuzzFeed and more than fifteen years working for other people, I could define my own lane. In my forties, it was time to start working for myself—and *being* myself.

CHAPTER TWENTY-NINE

A round the same time that I quit my job, we did another
egg retrieval—our fourth. The meds and injections now
felt routine; it hardly even seemed noteworthy that we were
doing another round of IVF, except that Matt was working
eighty-hour weeks, including a weekly trip to New York. He'd
been hired to be the host of *After Trek,* the aftershow for the
new *Star Trek: Discovery,* and it shot live on Sunday nights in
New York. So on Friday night after he left work—he was now
a writer on the sitcom *The Goldbergs*—he got on a plane, then
came back on the six A.M. flight on Monday morning and
went straight to work. We recorded *Eggcellent Adventure* on
Wednesday mornings because it was the only time during the
week that he was guaranteed to be around. It was a grueling
schedule, and even though he loved the work, he was miserable.

"I'm too stressed," he said. "I just don't think it's a good
time to do a retrieval."

"I'm forty," I said. "We're running out of time." We only
had one normal frozen embryo left, and I was worried that if

we transferred it and it didn't work, then the window when I could potentially make more normal embryos was rapidly closing.

So we went ahead with it, but it felt like one of those decisions where neither of us was totally happy. I was annoyed that Matt wasn't fully on board, that he had taken on so much work that it was literally draining us. It felt like we were on a road trip that had gone on too long, and we were bickering about finding a gas station, and I wanted to stop for the night and he wanted to keep going, and finally we pulled into a crappy motel on the side of the freeway where I wasn't able to sleep anyway because we could hear the couple next door having sex. Except we weren't on a road trip—we were talking about possibly creating another human life.

The day of the retrieval, having pumped myself full of meds for the previous two weeks, I was wheeled into the operating room, while Matt walked into what he referred to as the clinic's "jerk-off room" to collect the sperm that we'd need to fertilize my eggs.

The jerk-off room was a frequent topic of conversation on *Eggcellent Adventure.* Matt described it as almost comically unsexy, with a sad armchair covered with a disposable pad, a three-ring binder filled with pornographic DVDs, and some old *Playboys.* We'd heard from listeners who opted not to use the jerk-off room—some because they were Orthodox Jews, and they were having sex with a "fertility condom" instead, then rushing their specimen to their clinic within an hour. Another listener wrote in to ask for advice on setting up an in-home jerk-off room for her and her wife's friend, who was donating his sperm to them, and she asked what kind of vessel we thought was best for collection. We suggested a ramekin, and she henceforth deemed herself the "Ramekin Queer." But Matt had to use the jerk-off room, and just the thought of it seemed to make him depressed.

Going into the morning of the retrieval, my numbers looked good, and after the retrieval, Dr. Baek seemed cautiously optimistic. We ended up with five fertilized eggs—a lower number than we'd ever gotten, but at least something to work with. Now we just had to wait five or six days to see how many of the embryos would make it to the blastocyst stage.

That weekend was the last episode of Matt's stint as the host of *After Trek,* and I made the trip to New York to watch the show in person. It was taped in a studio on the far west side of Manhattan, near the Hudson Tunnel, a weirdly desolate neighborhood especially on a freezing Sunday afternoon. Going into the weekend, we had no idea how many embryos were still growing, and I kept checking my phone because I wasn't sure when we'd get word.

Finally, my phone rang. It was Dr. Baek. "None of your embryos made it to blastocyst," she said. "I'm so sorry."

"How . . . how is this possible?" I asked. I was pacing the hallway outside the studio, trying to keep my voice down and also trying not to cry.

"I know, it's really disappointing," she said. "The good news is, I'm confident that it's a sperm issue. So if you wanted to do another round, it's likely you wouldn't have the same problem, because Matt was on planes every week and so stressed."

"Okay," I said. I couldn't think about doing another round

right now. I hadn't even contemplated the possibility that *none* of the embryos would develop to the blastocyst stage—that had never happened before. Just when I thought I had seen every curveball that IVF treatment could throw at me, it managed to come up with yet one more. I was almost numb to the news—it just reminded me that there was absolutely nothing fair or rational about this process—and realized that I'd held out hope even when it didn't look like things were trending in the right direction. What was the point anymore of even holding on to *any* hope? I wondered. Every time I'd done that, I'd been devastated.

Matt was angry. "I *knew* we should have waited," he said. "I *told* you that my sperm wasn't going to be good."

"Can you just let me be upset about this without telling me that you were right? It's *really* annoying," I said. He skulked off as I tried not to cry. I didn't need to be reminded that Matt had been right. Shouldn't I be allowed to try without being made to feel like a failure for the attempt? I was angry at him, but I was mostly angry at our situation. All I had to show for nearly two years of fertility treatments was a podcast, a repaired uterus, and a lot of debt.

ONE OF THE things that is hard for people who aren't dealing with infertility to understand is how endless and hopeless it can feel when you're in the midst of it. Sure, there are those lucky people who only have to do one or two retrievals, their first transfer works, and whaddya know, they also had insurance coverage, so the whole thing cost them almost nothing. We did not have insurance coverage, and I was getting to the point where I felt like I was literally just throwing money away.

But it's also hard to know when to stop, because it's hard not to get swayed by the sunk cost fallacy—that is, thinking, *Well, I've spent SO MUCH money and time on this whole process already that I should just continue,* when in actuality, if you stop, you won't spend *any* more money or time, and if you keep going, you will *definitely* spend more money and time, and you still might not end up with a baby.

We told ourselves that every retrieval (after our second) was the last one. We were *done.* And after this retrieval, when none of the blastocysts had been normal, I wanted to be done, I really did, but there was a part of me that refused to believe that it wasn't going to work for us, despite all the evidence to the contrary. Deep down, I believed that our luck *had* to turn around. The whole time we were doing IVF, I hadn't truly allowed myself to consider all the possible outcomes; I had just assumed that we would end up with a baby that was biologically ours at the end. That was why we were doing this, right? That was what the doctors told us would happen. But I was choosing to ignore the fact that IVF does not give one single shit about how carefully you followed the protocols, or if you'd bought a car for a baby, or stayed at a job so you'd have maternity leave for a baby, or how much you thought you *deserved* this baby. IVF is here to say, "Who the hell do you think you are? You don't deserve this baby. You don't deserve *anything.*" IVF was going to make me its bitch and it was going to make sure I knew it.

We decided to do one more retrieval—just one more. This would be the last one, definitely, for sure, 100 percent. I was feeling confident going into it—after he had stopped traveling every weekend, Matt's sperm was looking a little better. IVF thought I was its bitch? I would make IVF *my* bitch.

We did the fifth retrieval and ended up with four blasto-cysts to biopsy for genetic testing. I was cautiously optimistic; we were already ahead of where we'd been on the last round, and I'd gotten at least one normal blastocyst from the previous three rounds. A few days later, I was sitting in my car after visiting a friend, about to drive off, when Dr. Baek called. She sounded subdued.

"So none of the embryos that we sent to be tested would be compatible with life," she said. "They were all abnormal." She paused. "I wasn't expecting this. I'm really sorry, Doree."

I wanted to be angry at someone, but I didn't know who. I knew Dr. Baek had done all she could. I couldn't be angry at Matt—it wasn't his fault that his sperm was "dumb." I could be angry at myself for thinking that IVF was foolproof, or for waiting so long to try to have kids, or for being born with a uterine septum, or or or . . . Or I could just be angry, full stop.

A year ago, I'd been impressed by the depths of the rage of the beautiful woman I'd encountered in a barre class, the grim-ness with which she was "working on herself" in front of the mirror, but I hadn't fully identified with her anger. Now, I real-ized, women are conditioned to believe that their anger not only isn't valid but also is something that needs to be con-tained or channeled into something productive. I was reject-ing that notion. I just wanted to acknowledge that what I was going through sucked, and I was allowed to be really fucking angry about it, and I wanted everyone else to know how angry I was, too.

But as I was allowing myself to be angry, I still had to con-front the reality that we might not end up with the baby I had convinced myself that we deserved. Instead of depressing me, though, this thought actually liberated me. What if we *just didn't have a child*? What would our lives look like? What would our marriage look like? What if the true "miracle" wasn't actually having the baby, but being at peace with however the so-called journey concluded?

"If we didn't have a kid," Matt said, "you know our lives would be easier."

"I *know* that," I said. I sighed. It almost felt transgressive to allow myself to think about a childless life that wasn't depressing but, rather, fulfilling. "We'd definitely be able to travel more."

"And get more dogs," he said.

"Dogs!" I said. "You know my fantasy is to have a huge piece of land where we just have a gajillion dogs running around."

"Well, that would be doable," he said. "I mean, maybe not *right* away. But we could start with, like, one other dog."

"And we'd definitely be able to sleep in more," I said. As I talked it through, I was warming to this plan. "Which would be a plus. And we'd have more money, and we wouldn't have to buy a big house because it would just be the two of us, and I wouldn't need my big dumb car, and I'd still be superclose with my nieces and nephew. I'd be the cool aunt!"

"You *are* the cool aunt," he said.

"I know. But I'd get to really lean into it," I said. "Plus, we'd never have to think about childcare."

This whole time, I'd been framing infertility treatments as the means to an end that I was sure I wanted. But now, I felt a weight lifting; it was so freeing to allow myself to be truly happy with the alternate version of my life. It reminded me of the period in my life when it felt like I was never going to meet a partner, and instead of letting that fear overtake me, I decided to try on the vision of my life as a single person, and that was comforting. Now I felt like I'd regained a tiny bit of control over a process that was almost completely outside of my control.

CHAPTER THIRTY

I decided to get a second opinion on our options, so I made an appointment for a phone call with a doctor from the Colorado Center for Reproductive Medicine, better known as CCRM, which is widely considered one of the best clinics in the country. I don't know what I was looking for, exactly, in that phone call, but I think I was hoping for something that no good doctor would tell me: *We can get you pregnant! Just sign here!*

Instead, the doctor I spoke to was perfectly straightforward. Yes, our poor results could have been because of my old eggs or Matt's dumb sperm, and if we did a retrieval at their clinic, we would both have to be on supplements that supposedly improved egg and sperm quality. But, he suggested, it was also possible that the lab at my current clinic was simply not as good as the CCRM lab. I hung up the phone even more uncertain about what to do than before. Was it pointless to put another $25,000 we didn't have on credit cards, plus travel to Colorado, for a retrieval when our last three had been failures?

Matt was adamant that this was *not* what we should do. "Enough!" he said. "Don't you think we've been through enough? Let's just transfer our last embryo and be done with it. And if it doesn't work, then we can have a lot of dogs."

The transfer itself felt anticlimactic, like I was just going through the motions: Go to clinic. Undress in bathroom and leave clothes in locker. Come out in hospital gown and lie on bed. Fill out forms. Take Valium. Watch Matt struggle to get into protective gear. Get wheeled into operating room. See embryo up on screen. Lie back while doctor inserts catheter. Watch embryo be deposited into uterus. Get dressed. Go home. Try not to think about whether cells are currently multiplying inside of me. Try not to think that every twinge of a sore boob or unusual fatigue means I'm pregnant. Insert progesterone suppositories into my vagina twice a day (I was given suppositories this time instead of shots, and even though suppositories are messy and kind of gross in their own way, I was extremely grateful to not have to be doing the butt shots again). Repeat, repeat, repeat.

My parents came to visit a few days later. At lunch, my mom asked if we'd thought about names yet. "Why would we do that?" I said. "It's not like this is going to work."

"Don't *say* that," Matt said. "You can't say that."

"Why not?" I said. I was feeling punchy. "It's not like anything I say or do now is going to make a difference, and I really don't think it worked."

My blood test was at the end of the week, the day before I was supposed to leave for a trip to Upstate New York, where Kate and I would be speaking at a retreat. The clinic's lab opened at 7:00 A.M., and I was the first one there. "Good luck," the phlebotomist said as the dark red blood dripped into the tubes.

"Thanks," I said. I wasn't feeling lucky. I wasn't even feeling cautiously optimistic. I was feeling like every last shred of hope had been sucked out of me.

The hours ticked by with no call from the clinic. After lunch, I headed to Target to get some last-minute supplies for the trip, like bug spray and sunscreen. I texted Matt to say I was worried that it wasn't a good sign that I hadn't heard from the clinic yet. "They probably call all of the positive tests first and leave the negative ones to later in the day," I wrote. As I sent the text off, my phone rang. It was Dr. Baek.

"Congratulations!" she said.

It took me a moment. Surely . . . she wouldn't be saying congratulations if it was bad news, right? But I couldn't quite wrap my head around the idea that it was *good* news. "Wait. No," I said. "You're *joking*."

"I'm not," she said. "You're pregnant. You're *very* pregnant." My HCG was high, over three hundred. I thought back to the blood test when my HCG had been six, and how I had held out hope that it would be viable. Now, there was no question that I was pregnant. Dr. Baek had said I was *extremely* pregnant! I hung up, dazed, still in the bug spray aisle. I selected a can of OFF! and called Matt. He didn't answer. "CALL ME," I texted, and headed to the cash register. He called back as I was paying.

"Hi," I whispered. "Guess what. I'm pregnant."

This time, I started crying. But for the first time since I'd started this long, horrible journey, they were actually tears of joy.

. . .

I HAD TEXTED my sister right after I called Matt. "OH MY GOD!!" she wrote back. "I knew it! I wrote down that I thought you were going to have a beta of 217!"

"It was higher than that!" I responded. "I'm *really* pregnant!"

It was hard to wrap my head around being pregnant. I didn't really feel any different. Of course, it was early—*very* early. Earlier than most people told their friends and family that they were pregnant, but because I'd already been so public about every step of the process, I felt like I could tell people.

And everyone was thrilled. "You're pregnant!" Kate said when we met up in New York the next night. We were sharing a room at a fancy hotel in Brooklyn the night before we would be driving upstate.

"I'm *pregnant*," I said. No matter how many times I said it, I still couldn't totally believe it. It had worked. All the money, all the meds, all the tears and the heartache—that part was over.

Except it wasn't, not really. I think lots of pregnant women, no matter how they got pregnant, are nervous about miscarriage in the first trimester, but I was borderline obsessed. It's estimated that up to 20 percent of confirmed pregnancies end in miscarriage, and the risk is five times higher for women over forty than women under thirty-five and slightly higher for IVF pregnancies. I became hyperaware of the week-by-week statistics for miscarriage and I fixated on certain pregnancy milestones: If I could make it to the detection of the heartbeat on an ultrasound, the miscarriage risk went down. If I made it to twelve weeks, the miscarriage risk went way down. Each day, I repeated a mantra I'd seen in the *Eggcellent Adventure* Facebook group: *Today, I am pregnant.* It didn't make me completely forget my miscarriage anxiety, but it did force me to live, ever so briefly, in the moment. Today, I was pregnant.

CHAPTER THIRTY-ONE

One Saturday when I was around five weeks pregnant, I went to an orientation at an animal shelter in the San Fernando Valley where I was thinking about volunteering. I sat through the presentation by the volunteer coordinator, then we were released to wander around the kennels and get a sense of what the shelter was like. As I assumed, it was grim: cage after cage of dejected-looking dogs, some clearly hyperanxious, some just seeming depressed. Would I be able to handle volunteering here? I wasn't sure. I had to use the bathroom, and when I wiped after peeing, there was bright red blood on the toilet paper.

"Oh god," I whispered. This was it—the miscarriage I had been bracing myself for. I tried to blot out as much blood as I could and hurried back to my car, where I called my clinic to speak to a nurse.

"Um, yeah, hi, I'm around five weeks pregnant, and I just saw some blood and I'm really nervous," I said, the words tumbling out of me.

The nurse seemed calm—maybe too calm. "Okay," she

said. "Spotting is very common in early pregnancy, especially IVF pregnancies. How much are you bleeding?"

"I don't know," I said. "Enough to notice? It seemed like a period, I guess."

"Put a pad on, and if you fill more than a pad an hour with blood, call us again," she said. "Again, this is very common and probably nothing to worry about."

"I still want to see Dr. Baek as soon as possible," I said. Suddenly, the threat of losing the pregnancy had made it seem deeply real. And I needed to do whatever I could to make sure that I wasn't going to lose it.

The next day, Matt and I went in to see Dr. Baek. I lay back on the exam table as she inserted the ultrasound wand into my vagina—it was too early to do an ultrasound on my belly— and I took a deep breath as she looked on the monitor. "There it is!" she said, calmly but triumphantly. "And look—we can already see the heartbeat!" She turned on the volume and I heard a rat-a-tat rhythm. "See that?" She pointed to a tiny vibrating speck on the screen. "That's the embryo. It's doing great!" She squinted at the screen again. "Sometimes the bleeding can be from a subchorionic hematoma, but I'm not seeing one," she said. "I can't really say why you were bleeding. It's possible that the progesterone was irritating your cervix, but I'm not really sure. Either way, you'll need to take it easy for the next few days, okay?"

I was relieved, to be sure, but the whole experience had scared me. It was a reminder of just how precarious those rapidly multiplying cells inside of me were. I still felt like the pregnancy itself wasn't *totally* real, or at least, that it could disappear at literally any minute. I know it was how I had to protect myself after so much heartache and disappointment, but it made me anxious.

While that bullet had been dodged, a few days later, my iced coffee just tasted . . . off. I drank a couple of sips of it and put it down in the cup holder in my car. *That's weird,* I thought. I usually slurped down my morning iced coffee in record time; since getting pregnant it was my only caffeine of the day, and I needed it, I thought, to function.

Then meat started to seem unappetizing, and then salad, and then one afternoon I was sitting in the living room with Matt when I suddenly felt awful. "I'm going to go lie down," I told him. "Really not feeling great." Then I threw up.

It wasn't like I didn't know anything about pregnancy nausea. My sister had had it really badly with both her kids, once puking in a cardboard box in her office because she knew she wouldn't make it to the bathroom in time. But I hadn't grasped the *totality* of pregnancy nausea, how it would come to dominate every moment of every day, that my baseline would be to feel queasy all day every day.

If you've never experienced constant nausea, I'm not sure there's a way to describe it that fully expresses how completely debilitating it is. Even if I wasn't actively throwing up, I felt like I was about to. The list of things I could eat without immediately puking got smaller and smaller. Toast, bagels with cream cheese, cereal, Saltines—that was pretty much it, and to drink, Gatorade or seltzer or water with an electrolyte packet dissolved in it. If I tried to drink plain water, I threw up. My doctor prescribed a medication called Diclegis that was supposed to mitigate the nausea, and it did, a bit. I still threw up and I still felt nauseated all the time, but just *slightly* less nauseated. But the medication also made me sleepy and foggy, like my brain was suddenly full of cotton batting, and I struggled to get out of bed.

Throughout all this, I'd heard from so many women on social media and through both podcasts who had had similar experiences—except they worked in offices, or retail jobs, or factories, or, really, anywhere that wasn't their home. They were women who were on their feet all day, women who dragged themselves to workplaces when they could barely get out of bed, women who were afraid of revealing their pregnancies for fear of being fired. I didn't have to deal with any of those things, and I thought about it every day. In the same way that I'm convinced if men got their periods, they would all get a week off every month, I'm convinced that if men got pregnant they would be allowed to take unlimited paid sick days with no repercussions. Hell, they would probably get a law passed that said they could take their entire pregnancies off work, fully paid.

"I think I need to do the podcast at my house for the foreseeable future," I told Kate. "I'm trying to minimize the amount of time I spend in the car." For the times that I couldn't avoid getting in the car, I had bought a package of barf bags that were now in the pocket of the driver's-side door. "Do you mind coming here?"

She did not. On pretty much a daily basis, I thought, *Thank God for Kate,* as I shuffled from the bedroom to the office so we could record the podcast, stopped in the kitchen for a slice of toast, and then shuffled back to the bedroom. I couldn't believe my naïveté about wanting to be pregnant at my *wedding*—that would have been an utter disaster—or how

I'd planned to get pregnant while I was still working at BuzzFeed. If I'd still been working in an office, I would have had to take medical leave.

Now I was getting very little done because I felt so sick, and Kate was covering for me. And yet millions of pregnant people every year are expected to just pretend like they're fine, because pregnancy nausea is usually the worst during the first trimester, which is also the trimester where most women are keeping the news of their pregnancy to themselves, because the odds of miscarriage are highest before the twelve-week mark. It plays into the pernicious expectation that women's suffering should not just be invisible, but also is barely worth acknowledging.

But we're used to that, aren't we? From the time we get our first periods, we're told explicitly and implicitly that the pain and emotions we feel around the time we get our periods are just "women's troubles." Again, I am 1,000 percent convinced that periods would be national holidays if cis men also got them, but since it's mostly just us gals (and trans men and nonbinary people who get periods!), we're supposed to act like it's cool! It's *totally cool;* let me just run this marathon and lead this board meeting while my insides are literally bleeding out of me, I have a splitting headache, and my stomach cramps are nothing short of debilitating. Really, NO BIG DEAL! DON'T MIND ME!

Another devastating version of this stigma surrounds miscarriage, because there has historically been just one way to experience a miscarriage, and that has been silently. But whose feelings are we protecting when we tell women not to tell friends and family that they're pregnant? A miscarriage is a horrible thing to endure alone, but when women haven't told anyone that they were pregnant, they don't have anyone to turn to when it happens. Not telling friends and family isn't just to protect the person who's experiencing the miscarriage; it's also to protect the feelings of the people who may not know the right thing to say, how to respond, or what to do. It's another way that women are told that their grief and their trauma shouldn't take up space. But now, I was taking up more space, both literally and figuratively. It seemed especially cruel of my body, after the gut-wrenching IVF process, to now be betraying me yet again. I wanted everyone to know how much it sucked.

So I began, hesitatingly at first and then more confidently, to post on Instagram about how I was feeling. You also don't see many women talking openly about pregnancy nausea, in large part because of the whole not-telling-people-you're-pregnant-too-early thing, but I recalled that Kate Middleton had been diagnosed with hyperemesis gravidarum, which was like pregnancy nausea on steroids. I was in a somewhat different situation, though: Thousands of people already knew I was pregnant, because I'd talked about it in great detail on *Eggcellent Adventure,* and people had been following my pregnancy since my fetus was literally just a few cells. So I wasn't hesitant because I was worried about revealing an early pregnancy, but because even though I was suffering, deep down I felt like I didn't have the right to complain after such a long and public struggle with infertility. I was still the person I'd been just a couple of months before who would have given anything to have pregnancy nausea—wasn't I? But did that mean my pregnancy would be forever defined by what had come before?

To my great relief, most people were extremely supportive, commiserating with me and offering up what had worked for them to quell the nausea. But not everyone. A woman wrote me on Instagram to say that she'd been a fan of mine—she had even supported our podcast on Patreon, paying each month to get bonus episodes. But she wanted me to know that she was *really* sick of hearing me complain about being pregnant. Didn't I know that things were going to get so much worse after the baby was born? I didn't know what I was in for, she told me, so really, I should just shut up now.

She was a certain kind of person who I like to call the "just you wait"ers. They're the people who don't allow you to live in the moment—whether you're trying to celebrate or complain about something. "You think things are good/bad now? *Just you wait*—you have [insert some horrible-sounding thing here] coming up." If I'm being generous, I would say that this impulse seems to stem from people's desires to be genuinely helpful, but I actually think it's rooted in the tendency some people have to remind you that they have suffered, and you will suffer too. It's a way of centering the conversation back to them.

To be visible and vocal is to be criticized, I reminded myself. Women have been attacked online much more severely for much less. I was lucky that the worst I was getting was some random person's bitterness. In the past, I would have spiraled, but now, I simply blocked her. This was about her, not me. I was glad I could finally see that.

CHAPTER THIRTY-TWO

I stopped feeling nauseated gradually. First I went for a couple of days without vomiting, then a week, then ten days, and then, around the sixteen-week mark, I realized that I wanted to eat something other than a carb. And then I started to feel *amazing*. My pregnancy became the kind of pregnancy that I'd heard people talk about, that I thought only happened to people in their twenties who made pregnancy look effortless: My skin glowed, my hair thickened. I went to prenatal yoga twice a week and Pilates and worked out with weights at the gym; I felt good in my body in a way that I never had before. I'd heard people talk about how, when they were pregnant, their bodies didn't feel like their own, that they basically had a parasite living inside of them. I did not feel this way. People stopped me on the street to tell me I looked beautiful. Friends commented on my Instagram photos to say how great I looked.

I felt guilty for relishing the attention paid to my body. You would think that suddenly having an enormous protruding stomach would have made me feel even more insecure, but it did the opposite; the only other time I'd felt so confident in my body was after the breakup with Jon, when Revenge Jacket Doree entered my life—not exactly a healthy time. But now I had been given *permission* to have an enormous stomach. "You have a *perfect* basketball stomach," a friend said, a note of envy in her voice.

"What does that mean?" I asked.

"You know, skinny legs and a nice round tummy poking out." I felt gross that on some level, this delighted me. Still, it was hard not to internalize the message: Have the basketball stomach, but don't get *too* fat, because then how are you supposed to "lose the baby weight" and "get your body back"? I found these phrases to be the most insidious. What did that mean, exactly, to "get your body back"? Where had your body *gone*? Wasn't your body always right here, doing exactly what it was supposed to be doing? In the country that I'm planning on leading, in addition to getting a week off for your period, unlimited paid sick leave, and a year of parental leave, I'll issue an executive order that the bodies of people who have just created another human inside their own bodies should be celebrated, worshipped, coddled for at least a year, no matter what they look like. Preferably forever, but we can start with a year.

For me, the expectations of how to perform pregnancy were partly wrapped up in my age. I was forty-one when I got pregnant, which was old to have a first child even for my cohort of women who had had kids "late." There's a certain kind of pregnant influencer who tends to be twenty-five, gorgeous, and already has two kids, who has someone (her Instagram husband?) take ethereal photos of her in a low-cut prairie dress, standing in a field, her long hair flowing down her back. These moms, who are almost entirely white, love to post pictures of their nurseries-in-progress, carefully curated rooms in neutral browns and pinks.

I related to these women . . . not at all. Where were the women like me who were over forty, having their first kid, and amused at (and somewhat befuddled by) these influencers who were young enough to be our children?

EARLY IN MY second trimester, right around the time that I started feeling less nauseated, I decided that I wanted to hire a doula to assist in my labor and birth. A birth doula is someone who helps prep you for your birth, comes to your house when you go into labor, and is with you through the delivery. They're supposed to be your advocates with whomever and wherever you're giving birth, whether it's with doctors and nurses at a hospital, with a midwife in a birthing center, or at home. It sounded great—someone who'd been to dozens if not hundreds of births who'd be able to support me at an incredibly vulnerable time, and hopefully also make sure my husband kept his wits about him. Friends who had given birth before me were adamant that having a doula helped them, and I figured I could use all the help I could get.

The first one I called seemed pleasant enough, and after a few minutes of my asking her about her experience, she started asking me questions. Like: "What are you picturing for your birth?"

I was stumped. I knew there was no right or wrong way to give birth, but she was waiting expectantly for an answer. I got the feeling that to her, the right answer was *any* kind of vision for my birth at all. But after so much struggle to even get to the point where I was wearing distressed Madewell maternity jeans with the waistband that stretched over my stomach, the idea of actually giving birth and having a real, live child still seemed abstract. I had spent so much time, money, and mental energy trying to get pregnant—*that* seemed like the endgame. It's like focusing so much on the wedding and not the marriage: I had been so hyperfocused on just getting pregnant, that even the pregnancy—let alone the birth and the idea of having a child—felt beyond my comprehension.

In a Facebook group for women who were due around the same time as me, people talked about delayed cord clamping, walking epidurals, laboring in tubs, the positions they wanted to be in during the birth. We were months away from giving birth but they were already discussing what to take to the hospital—what kind of essential oils would they have in their diffuser? What was on their labor playlist? Were they going to have a videographer at the birth? These questions overwhelmed me. I scrolled through the comments on these posts, growing increasingly anxious but not able to look away.

And now, I was being asked this question in real life. I took a breath. "I'm really just focused on having a healthy baby," I said.

"But you know, you are allowed to think about what kind of birth you want to have," she said.

"I guess," I said. I didn't like that this woman was acting like she had the right to give me permission to come up with an ideal birth. And maybe it was the IVF talking, but I really *didn't* have a vision for my birth. I felt like she wanted me to say that I would labor at home in a tub, then be rolled into the hospital in a wheelchair wearing a flower crown and smelling of lavender, smiling beatifically at the nurses as I felt my contractions. At the very least, she was probably hoping I would say I wanted to pay her to make pills out of my placenta. (No judgment if that's your thing but no thanks, not for me.)

To be fair, it was slightly misleading to say I had *no* vision for my birth. I'd had several friends who'd been induced—which is when labor doesn't start on its own, and for medical reasons (usually) the doctor wants to get things moving, so they give you drugs to jump-start labor—and the induction had gone on for so long that they'd ended up with an unplanned cesarean section, having to be rushed into the OR, shell-shocked from everything that had happened, unable to revel in the first few moments with their newborn. That was the birth that I was sure I *didn't* want. It just sounded so miserable, hanging out in the hospital for hours or even days while your body tried to respond to various drugs that they were pumping into you, maybe even being in active labor for hours on end, only to end up in the operating room getting cut open to get your baby out.

I said this to the doula hopefully, like this "vision" of my birth would be sufficient.

"You know, just because you did IVF, you don't only need to want a healthy baby," she said, pressing me again.

"Okay," I said. "Listen, it's been really great talking to you, but I actually have to jump off. I'll let you know if I have any other questions." I hung up. It felt like the specter of IVF was going to permeate the entirety of my pregnancy, coming up at times that I wasn't anticipating it, and sending me back to the place that I was trying to forget.

I told Cynthia, my therapist, about my conversation with the doula. "Am I ever going to stop feeling like an IVF mom?" I asked.

"It's hard to move past it, I know," she said. "What does that bring up for you, though?"

I thought about her question for a moment. "I guess I feel like my pregnancy has an asterisk next to it, and I'm always trying to feel like a 'real' pregnant person," I said.

"Well, you are a 'real' pregnant person," she said, "but I don't think you necessarily *need* to 'move past it.' It's always going to be a part of your story."

"You're right," I said. "And I'm not embarrassed about it. If anything, I feel like I should have a gold medal next to my pregnancy, not an asterisk."

Or maybe my resistance to developing a birth plan had more to do with being an "old" mom than having done IVF. If I were giving birth at, say, age twenty-six, I might still think that I had some control over any of this. But being older, coupled with having done IVF, made me all too aware that when it comes to our bodies, the best-laid plans inevitably go awry. What was the point, I wondered, of making a whole elaborate birth plan, only to see it discarded once you needed a blood transfusion, or the baby got stuck, or the pain you so confidently thought you'd be able to get through without meds suddenly got so overwhelming that you felt like you couldn't get the epidural put in quickly enough? It seemed like a recipe for disappointment, and I had already had enough experience with getting my hopes up. The birth would just be a continuation of everything else I'd already had to accept as being out of my control—which, I suspected, would continue long after I gave birth, anyway. Why not get used to it now?

CHAPTER THIRTY-THREE

Matt likes to say that he doesn't like to plan, but he does like to be prepared. He says it comes from being a Boy Scout—and his response to my fear of having an unplanned C-section was that I should just plan the C-section. His reasoning was that if we scheduled it, then we'd know ahead of time, and there would be zero risk of ending up unexpectedly in the OR.

This seemed like flawed logic to me. If I scheduled a C-section, then yes, I would have zero risk of an unplanned C-section, but I would also have a zero percent chance of having a vaginal birth. We discussed my birth plan or lack thereof with Dr. Brown, my OB, a matter-of-fact woman with curly brown hair that always seemed damp, like she had just rushed to our appointment from a postdelivery shower.

"I can't guarantee anything," she said, "but I will try."

I liked Dr. Brown. She never once uttered the words *geriatric pregnancy* or said anything about being an older mom; the only times it came up were when I pressed her on it. Would I need an induction at thirty-nine weeks to avoid stillbirth, like some doctors were recommending for patients over a certain age? She shrugged and said that she didn't think the evidence for doing it was particularly compelling, and besides, even though I was forty-one, I was otherwise healthy.

"So when would you say this baby has to come out?" I asked.

"Probably at forty-two weeks, I'd say it was time," she said.

AND SO I woke up the morning of my due date, April 22, 2019, feeling great. I was healthy, if slightly uncomfortable, but I hadn't developed any of the physical ailments of pregnancy that I'd been warned about, like varicose veins or sciatica or hemorrhoids. I was having trouble sleeping—I was waking up in the early morning hours, around three or four A.M., and was often unable to go back to sleep for an hour or two, if at all—but otherwise, I felt pretty good. And at the end of my thirty-ninth week, when I had gone in for my ultrasound, the ultrasound tech told me that the baby was still firmly, cozily pretty far up in my uterus. He hadn't "dropped," which is when the baby makes his way closer to the cervix in preparation to leave the womb. He seemed to be in no hurry, she said. Meanwhile, Matt was hopeful that we'd be able to go to opening night of the new Marvel movie, *Avengers: Infinity War;* I had tickets to see one of my favorite riot grrrl bands, Bikini Kill, perform three days past my due date. (As one of my friends put it: "It would be *so* punk rock to go into labor at a Bikini Kill show," but it also seemed like it could be, I don't know, messy?)

I had an appointment with Dr. Brown that morning, and before we left the house, I snapped a picture in the mirror. I was wearing a stretchy black dress and sneakers, and cradling my bump. I captioned it, "Bump pic but make it art . . . btw today is my due date. He's still in there." I felt relaxed. I liked my pregnancy glow, and I wanted to enjoy it.

At the doctor's office, I maneuvered myself onto the exam table for my ultrasound, and breathed a little sigh of relief as the ultrasound tech checked the baby. Matt, who was sitting on a chair at the foot of the table, and I stared up at the monitor. Our baby was right there, looking pretty content, just chilling in that cozy amniotic fluid. Was he sucking his thumb? He was.

Everything looked perfect, she said. Except . . . she frowned. "Hmm," she said. "Uh-oh." The radiologist was a honey-blond Russian woman, not given to chitchat. I preferred the other radiologist, who was French, even though she had once matter-of-factly pointed out my baby's "pee pee" on the ultrasound and made a joke about it being large because my dad is Israeli (gross). As I lay on the exam table, the warm gel on my now-mountainous stomach ("This is Beverly Hills," the French radiologist had told me, "we warm the gel"), I didn't like the sound of "uh-oh."

"Your amniotic fluid is low," she said, with not a word minced. "Dr. Brown is going to send you to the hospital. You will be induced tonight." If your fluid is low, your placenta can start to fail, and your baby will die.

Even as she said it, I didn't believe it. Surely my doctor would look at the rest of the scans and determine that this one factor of my fluid being low didn't necessitate an urgent trip to the hospital?

"When you say 'low,'" I said, "what do you mean exactly?"

"Normal is eight or above," she said. "You are at a 5.9."

And a few minutes later, as I was hooked up to a stress test machine, Dr. Brown looked through the results of the ultrasound and agreed with the Russian radiologist.

"Okay, so you're going to have to go into the hospital tonight, and we'll start the induction," she said.

"That's our only option?" I asked.

"Look, if this had happened at thirty-seven weeks, I might have told you to go get fluids at the hospital and then we could reevaluate, but since you're at forty weeks, and also you're forty-one, I'm going to say that yes, this is your only option," she said. She had once told us she went to SoulCycle every morning at six before coming into work and I liked to imagine that sometimes, after an especially long night at the hospital, she just went straight to SoulCycle to sweat it out.

"I just really didn't want to be induced," I said.

"I know," she said. "I'm sorry."

There was a brief silence.

Matt said, "I told you we should have scheduled a C-section—"

"Not now," I said to him. "I don't want to discuss this right now." I was going to be induced and that was that. "Okay, so, tonight," I said to the doctor. "Does it matter what time?"

"Not really, but I would go around eight, after the shift change. I'll call them now and let them know to expect you." Matt and I drove home, dazed but also slightly frantic. I'd started packing my hospital bag a couple of weeks before, but now I threw more stuff into tote bags: my own hospital gown, slippers, headphones, leggings, a caftan, a toothbrush, a Bluetooth speaker for the seven-hour labor and delivery playlist that, despite my eye-rolling, I had ended up making. (I had drawn the line at a diffuser, however.) I had a pillow for Matt, and coconut water and apple juice. We were as ready as we were going to be.

IT FELT WEIRD to be pulling up to the hospital when I wasn't in labor. I'd been picturing something very different—starting labor at home, and having to make the call about when to head over to the hospital. Maybe we'd mistime it and I'd already be in active labor when we got there! Maybe Matt would drive up to the emergency room, tires squealing, and I'd be taken up to labor and delivery in a wheelchair. Instead, we parked, took all our bags out of the trunk, and took the elevator up to labor and delivery.

Our room was small, but it was private, and I changed into my gown and tried to get comfortable. A nurse attached a strap around my enormous stomach and told me that they'd be continuously monitoring the baby's heart rate, and I couldn't roll over to the side or the monitor would slip off. A nurse explained that they would be inserting a medication called Cervidil into my vagina; after around twelve hours, my cervix would hopefully be dilated to three or four centimeters, at which point I would either go into active labor on my own or they could start an IV of Pitocin, which would get my contractions going, and then my baby would come flying out of me.

The first challenge came when they tried to examine my cervix to see how much I was already dilated. The nurse inserted her fingers into my vagina and tears came to my eyes. It felt like someone was ramming something between the size of a wooden spoon and an eighteen-wheeler deep inside me, then trying to go deeper. "That . . . that really hurts," I said.

"Hmm, okay," the nurse said—not like she didn't believe me, but also not exactly like she did. The Cervidil came in a pouch with a string attached that would be inserted in my vagina. As I suspected would happen, she had some trouble getting it in. "Try to get some rest," she said, and the weird thing was that she was serious.

In the meantime, Matt was trying to expand the small sofa so he could lie down, but the only way to extend it blocked the door to the bathroom. We decided we would leave the bathroom door slightly open—but that also meant that the door wouldn't close, either. If you're someone who gets off on the idea of peeing in the dark in an open-back gown while your husband snores three feet away from you, then this setup might have been exciting, but since that is not a specific fantasy of mine, it was just annoying.

On the tour of the hospital, they'd taken us into one of the labor and delivery rooms and made a big deal about how there was a tub in the bathroom, so if you were someone who was into the idea of laboring in a tub, then you'd want this room. At the time, I thought, sure, laboring in a tub sounds kind of cool, in an *I'm not enough of a hippie to give birth at home but I can get down with laboring in a tub* kind of way. Now that I was actually at the hospital, but nowhere near going into labor, I had no desire to get anywhere near a tub. All I wanted to do was sleep, but that was impossible. And I couldn't feel anything happening inside me. I lay down on the bed and tried not to move.

. . .

THE NEXT MORNING, Matt went downstairs to get coffee. I'd
barely slept, since every time I tried to get comfortable, the
monitor slid off me and a nurse came in to readjust it. "The
room across the hall is open," Matt said. "It's *much* nicer than
this one. It has a huge window."

"Ask them if we can switch," I said.

"Ask who?" he said.

"I don't know. The person at the desk?"

"I don't want to bother them," he said.

"Oh come on," I said. "This is the time to bother someone!"

"Not gonna do it," he said.

So when my nurse came in a few minutes later, I asked, in
my nicest I-know-this-is-totally-against-policy-but-I'm-going-
to-ask-anyway voice, if we could move across the hall.

"We usually don't move people," she said. She had a gruff
demeanor. I must have looked really pathetic lying there,
though, because then she said, "But I'll ask."

We moved. I took a kind of grim satisfaction in feeling like
I had negotiated a room upgrade at the Best Western. It turned
out that was the only satisfaction that was going to be had
right then. The new room may have been bigger and brighter,
but my cervix didn't seem to care. My doctor came by to see
why things weren't progressing and informed me that I had "a
cervix like Fort Knox" and that it was the "most impenetrable
cervix" she'd seen in fifteen years of practice; I had to be given
fentanyl to be able to tolerate the cervical checks, and even
then they were still incredibly painful; to get a Foley balloon

in, which is supposed to force your cervix open with an actual balloon, I had to have an epidural. A full day had gone by, and I had dilated barely three centimeters. I was supposed to, at that point, be at ten. The next morning they put me on Pitocin, a drug that's supposed to jump-start contractions, but nothing was jump-started, and eventually, forty hours into being at the hospital, my doctor informed me that they had done everything they could, but she was getting concerned about fever and my uterus overheating, which sounded unpleasant for everyone, and my contractions were barely perceptible on the monitor and still very far apart, and it didn't seem like the baby wanted to come out on his own. I was going to have a C-section.

From there everything happened very quickly. I was wheeled into the OR, and in the OR I started shaking uncontrollably, which they had not warned me was going to happen, and Matt was holding my hand and reassuring me that everything was going to be okay, and it felt like I was shaking on the operating table forever but it was really only about twenty minutes. I couldn't feel anything, but my insides were outside of my body and then, through the sheet, they held the baby up, and I exclaimed, "It's a baby!" Then I passed out.

CHAPTER THIRTY-FOUR

He looked like a Henry, we decided that first night, alone with the baby in the hospital room. He was sleeping in a clear-sided bassinet, his thin cotton hospital cap on top of a shock of black hair. I was hooked up to an industrial-strength breast pump, trying to convince my boobs to produce something—anything—so I could feed him. Finally, I was able to get some drops of liquid, but it looked brownish. "It's just a little blood—we call it a rusty pipe. It's fine to feed that to him," one of the nurses reassured me. *Gross*, I thought. When would I get "real" milk? I'd heard stories of women who were "overproducers," meaning that their breasts made so much milk that their babies gagged because of how quickly it came out and they ended up with multiple freezer chests full of bags of breast milk, but I wanted to just be producing *something*.

And I was still in a lot of pain, even though I was taking Percocet and Tylenol every few hours. In the morning, when they removed my catheter, I would have to go to the bathroom on my own. It turned out that just getting to the bathroom, which was only a few feet away, was a production, because it hurt to get out of bed, and it hurt to walk, and it hurt to sit down on the toilet and to get up. And then once I was finally on the toilet, I couldn't pee. I could feel the pee in my bladder, I *really* had to go, and yet, it wasn't coming out. I sat on the toilet, tears welling in my eyes. I couldn't pee, I could barely produce milk, I couldn't even sit up on my own.

When I'd woken up in the recovery room after the C-section, a nurse had put Henry on my chest, and he had attempted to nurse, but he couldn't get a good latch on my nipple. "Your nipples are flat—that's why he's having trouble," she said. "We'll have you use a nipple shield." I had the vague notion that this was the vaunted "skin to skin" contact that everyone talked about as being so important in bonding with the baby, but I could barely keep my eyes open. Now, in the hospital room, the nurse showed me how to use the nipple shield so he'd be able to latch. It was a small piece of plastic that suctioned on to my areola and had a little fake nipple that went over my nipple, with a few holes poked in the top so the milk would come out. I had trouble with this, too: I couldn't get the shield to stick on my nipple, and it seemed like even once my milk started flowing—albeit slowly—he wasn't getting that much of it.

I'd heard other moms talk about feeling so overcome with love when they first met their children, and instantly feeling bonded with them as though their new baby had immediately filled a hole in their lives. So I just assumed it was something that automatically happened to everyone. But I didn't feel that, exactly. I knew I loved Henry, and I was amazed by him and the fact that he had just been lifted out of my body. And of course, I was enormously grateful for him. But more than anything else, I felt overwhelmed. Here was this tiny, completely helpless human who was now completely dependent on me, and I didn't know the first thing about taking care of him. I couldn't even nurse him properly.

Was I supposed to have some kind of primal mother instinct that would click on? If I was, it hadn't clicked on yet. Maybe something was wrong with me. *How did everyone know exactly what to do?* I thought, getting slightly panicked. What if he cried and I couldn't console him? How would I know if he was hungry or sad or in pain? No one had told me that in the aftermath of the birth, I would feel so completely at sea.

What if, after everything we had gone through, I wasn't able to bond with my baby? What if I wasn't cut out to be a mother at all?

CHAPTER THIRTY-FIVE

Henry slept a lot the first couple of weeks of his life. His pediatrician had told me to exclusively breastfeed him to establish my supply and to make sure he didn't get too accustomed to a bottle, so if he wasn't asleep, he was on the boob. But breastfeeding hadn't become much easier than it initially had been those first couple of days in the hospital. I was still using a nipple shield, fumbling to get it on while Matt held Henry before placing him on my lap. Then he would scrabble around for my nipple with his little mouth and try to latch. If he didn't latch right away, I would try to adjust the angle of his head, or squeeze my nipple to try to get it into his mouth. But most of the time, even when he did latch, it was incredibly painful—I winced every time he suckled—and sometimes tears came to my eyes.

My breasts also got clogged constantly. A clog is like a very painful knot in your breast that can show up anywhere—sometimes it was on my underboob, sometimes it was by my armpit, sometimes it was practically at my sternum. Wherever it was, I would try to unclog it by pressing down on it as Henry nursed, which was doubly painful.

I googled "what to do when your boob is clogged," and the internet told me to get on all fours, with Henry underneath me, and dangle my breast into his mouth, while simultaneously pressing on the clog. I set him up on our bed and got on my hands and knees. He started screaming. I had never felt more kinship with a cow.

One night, my breasts were in so much pain that I couldn't sleep. I tried applying a warm compress to them, which didn't help, and then the internet said I could try a cold compress, so I took an ice pack out of the freezer, stood in front of my bathroom mirror, and put it directly on my breast. It felt good. I held it there for a few minutes, and then it started to feel really, really cold—almost burning. "Shit," I muttered as I removed the compress and looked in the mirror. I had given myself what looked like a third-degree burn, so now I was in the pain of still having a clog *and* having the skin on my breast essentially burned off. Under normal circumstances, I probably would have freaked out more than I did, but because I was so exhausted and overwhelmed and just so sick of having to deal with my boobs constantly, all day, every day, that a third-degree boob burn seemed like just one more thing in the pile of crap I needed to deal with.

I slathered some Neosporin on it and covered it with a bandage and tried to sleep.

A COUPLE OF DAYS LATER, we took Henry to the doctor for his two-week checkup. The pediatrician put him on the scale and frowned. "Hmm," she said. "He still isn't back to birth weight."

"That's bad, I guess?" I said.

"Well, by now we usually like to see them get back to

their birth weight, yes," she said. "How's the breastfeeding going?"

"I wouldn't say great," I said. "I'm still using the nipple shields and he has trouble latching, and because of the shields I can't really tell how much he's getting."

"Okay," she said. "So starting immediately I'd like you to start giving him bottles a few times a day, so you have a better idea of how much food he's actually getting."

I felt terrible. My inability to successfully breastfeed was affecting my baby's development. Before Henry was born, I had told myself that I wouldn't be one of those moms who became obsessed with breastfeeding above all else; I firmly believed that "fed is best," and we'd given Henry some formula in the hospital while my milk still hadn't fully come in. But breastfeeding also felt like something that I *should* know how to do, one of those motherly instinct things that you were just supposed to pick up right away. Not being able to breastfeed my baby was yet another way in which I felt like I wasn't measuring up. That must have been why he was sleeping so much—he was *hungry.*

When we got home, Matt sat down on the couch in our office and I handed him a bottle. Henry started wailing; he wasn't able to immediately latch on to the bottle. "He's starving," Matt said, and tears came to his eyes. "We've been starving him." Then he was fully sobbing. "I feel awful," he said.

"We're doing the best we can," I said. I couldn't help but think this was meant as an implicit judgment of me and my motherly instincts. Surely I should have known that he wasn't getting enough food—shouldn't I? But how was I to know? And we had caught it at the doctor before things had gotten dire. Henry finally latched on to the bottle and drank the whole thing.

EVERYONE SAYS THE sleeplessness of having a newborn is unlike anything they'd ever experienced, but in the same way that I had heard about pregnancy nausea but hadn't been able to *really* conceive of what it felt like, I had had no idea how waking up four times or more each night to feed a newborn, fumbling in the dark for a nipple shield, praying that he would actually latch and eat, and then not being able to fall back asleep *really* felt.

It's not just that I was exhausted in those first few weeks and months after having Henry; it was that the thought of just leaving the house seemed incredibly overwhelming. Impossible, even. Undoubtedly this was in part because of my C-section—truly, I never realized how much I actually used my abs until I had completely lost the use of them. Just getting out of bed was a tears-inducing pain; I had to roll over to my side and then sort of shimmy myself up on my elbow, swing my legs around, wince, and then slowly stand up and shuffle to the bathroom. I felt lingering pain that was not acute, but affected everything I did, in a way that was entirely foreign to me. It was there in every step I took, every time I wanted to reach up to get something down from a shelf, every time I got dressed and saw the bandaged scar above my pubic bone. I had thought that once I had the baby I would begin to reclaim my body from the visitor of the last nine months, but instead I felt more estranged from my body than before. When you think about it, of course it made sense: My internal organs had been temporarily removed, and another human who'd been gestating in there for the better part of a year was also removed, and now he lived with us. I was so focused on keeping this new human alive that I almost forgot that my body had undergone major surgery. I needed to be kind to it.

CHAPTER THIRTY-SIX

Before I had Henry, my impression of motherhood was that babies were demanding little creatures, but it was no problem to, say, take a newborn to a restaurant and have them sleep in the stroller, or swing by someone's house for dinner with the baby asleep in the car seat, or hang out with friends with your baby strapped adorably to your body in a carrier. Once I had a newborn, though, I realized that this is true only for a very small—let's say, infinitesimally small—segment of parents, and it is these parents who are ruining things for the rest of us.

What no one tells you is that taking a small baby on a picnic, or to a happy hour, or really, anywhere outside your home is actually a huge pain in the ass. You wouldn't know it, though, from following some new moms on Instagram. It's not news that people present their "best" selves, or at least, their carefully curated selves, on social media, and that people's Instagram feeds do not reflect reality. I knew this, and was occasionally guilty of it myself, and yet. AND. YET. I couldn't help but look at these photos and not only think *Why am I* not *taking my week-old baby to that happy hour/picnic/beach day?* but also

Why do I have no desire *to take my week-old baby to that happy hour/picnic/beach day?*

Because if you follow a certain kind of parent on Instagram with a small child, you would be forgiven if you thought that all new mothers (and some fathers) do is have picnics. You know the kinds of photos I'm talking about: a family lying on a blanket in a park, their babe cooing as the parents beam at their perfect spawn. Or the pictures of the moms sitting in a park wearing a long flowy dress while their baby sucks contentedly from their breast. Or a picnic on a beach with a baby, or a picnic on a magical roof deck at sunset with a baby, the city lights twinkling in the distance.

One mom I know posted a picture on Instagram literally one week after giving birth to her second child that said "Baby's first happy hour!" with a *Bon Appetit* Test Kitchen–level cheese board in the background. I was in awe and slightly jealous: At one week postpartum I was still in mesh panties, taking painkillers, and barely getting out of bed. I was struggling to nurse and pump and was staring down the barrel of a schedule that went roughly like this: Baby wakes up, change baby's diaper, feed baby, try to put baby down for another nap, start crying forty-five minutes later because he will not sleep. Repeat ad nauseam. I was also lucky if I ate a gram of protein each day. The thought of leaving the house, and drinking wine and eating cheese, was not just completely outside the realm of possibility, but also seemed vaguely nauseating.

Another thing I never really comprehended before I gave birth was the significance of the diaper bag. Surely it just entailed a bag . . . with diapers. Maybe some wipes? How complicated could that be? Couldn't I just use the Madewell tote I already had? Well. It turns out that a diaper bag also needs to have a change of clothes (or two), a changing pad, and a roll of baggies to dispose of poopy diapers. If you're bottle-feeding, it should have a prepared bottle or at least some formula. You of course need a couple of burp cloths and a bib or two. Don't forget the pacifier, but you'll probably need an extra just in case it goes missing, which it tends to do, because pacifiers are the socks of baby life—they just go missing. (Don't even get me started on baby socks.) You can literally be staring at a pacifier and it will disappear in front of your very eyes. It's like you've learned how to be a magician without even realizing it. Also, the pacifier will, 100 percent of the time, go missing at the exact moment that your baby has a complete meltdown, often in the one public place you ever take your baby when he or she is four weeks old, which is the doctor's office. (That is, unless you are an Instagram influencer who takes their perfectly chill baby to happy hours.)

In my case, the diaper bag also needed to have a nipple shield, just in case I forgot the bottle or the formula that I was supposed to have put in there, but inevitably, the day I forgot the bottle or the formula was also the day that I forgot the nipple shield, and it was also the day that Henry was getting his two-month shots, and it was also the day that his pediatrician was running over an hour late in the afternoon right around the time that Henry was starving. It's the Murphy's Law of diaper bags: The more urgent the situation, the more likely you are to have forgotten something absolutely crucial. (See also: baby having a huge poop blowout when you don't have a change of clothes with you.)

But even if you get the diaper bag sorted, and you want to actually leave the house, everything still has to be perfectly timed, because no one told you that when people say babies "sleep all the time," what they really mean is that babies sleep in increments of anywhere from thirty to ninety minutes, you just don't know which increment it's going to be until they wake up.

So as I got used to having Henry around, I regarded the photos of moms picnicking at the park with their babies with even more skepticism. Who were these moms who were able to magically engineer their babies to be awake when they needed them to be, make sure they didn't poop everywhere, and keep their babies generally content?

I had to wonder to what extent an influencer mom might feel like she needed to perform for her Instagram followers, to put on a show that she could still be the pretty, high-powered career woman balancing kids and an enviable social life. But maybe this particular photo was the only one she'd taken all day where the baby wasn't screaming and the toddler wasn't pouting. Maybe she had Facetuned her dark circles and her smile was fake. But none of that mattered, right? Because the end result projected *I've got this,* in a way that at that point, I most certainly did not. And while I looked at it and was slightly envious, I more just thought: *Wow, that seems* exhausting.

I still didn't feel like I had a mother's instinct—just the instinct to second-guess myself. And besides, so far, I hadn't found anything instinctual about motherhood. If anything, it felt more like a class that I was constantly behind in, and the professor never showed up to office hours—the professor being a twelve-pound person who still needed my help to burp. There was nothing instinctual about knowing how to put a baby to sleep, or how often he should sleep, or how much he should eat. More than once I wondered how the fuck the human race ever survived. Someone must have had some instincts very early on—a kind of cavewoman proto-Pinterest mom, who made the other cavewomen put bonnets made out of woolly mammoth fur on their babies so they wouldn't get cold.

ONE DAY, when Henry was around five weeks old, I stood in front of the full-length mirror in my bedroom, a long, stretchy piece of fabric wrapped around my waist and over my shoulders. It was the first time since the C-section that I'd felt like my body was ready to have a baby strapped to me. I placed Henry in the wrap carefully, pulling fabric up over his legs and torso. He squirmed a bit, and I rubbed his back and whispered, "Shhh, it's okay," and he quieted.

I walked around the house, feeling the warmth of his body against mine, his little head turned to one side, resting on my chest. He felt so snug and safe. *I* was making him feel snug and safe. Soon he fell asleep.

My year of yes had, with Henry's birth, given way to my year of no thanks. And yet, I was starting to feel more at ease with myself, and comfortable in the choices I was making, than I ever had when I was spending so much time—with men, at work, with friends—trying to be the "cool" girl, worrying that I was missing out on something. Now, I was doing what was right for me, what was right for Henry, what was right for us as a family. If ever there was a moment when I felt like I had grown, this was it.

Maybe the picnics and park hangs could wait, I thought. Maybe everything I needed was right here.

CHAPTER THIRTY-SEVEN

"How's he doing?" I texted my mom around halfway through the flight.

"Good," she responded. "Just went down for a nap."

I was on a plane to Orlando, where Kate and I would be speaking at a podcast conference. It would be my first night away from Henry since he was born; he was three and a half months old. Since Matt and I don't have family in Los Angeles— or anywhere nearby—we'd enlisted the help of my parents while I was gone, since Matt would have to work.

I hadn't ever really thought about the precariousness of our situation in L.A. until Henry came along. Suddenly, what had felt like an exciting adventure—moving across the country! marrying an amazing person! having a baby!—started to feel a little scary. Matt's parents lived in Florida; mine lived in Boston. My brother was in Connecticut, my sister in Texas. I knew we were hardly the first people to have this issue; lots of my friends in L.A. were transplants. But I still hadn't quite wrapped my head around feeling like a little island out here in California. My parents were thankfully still healthy, and as

THANKS FOR WAITING   271

long as we were willing to pay for a plane ticket, they were happy to come out to L.A. to stay with Henry. But even though they were healthy, they were still getting older, and anyway, coming to L.A. regularly to babysit just wasn't feasible. And, god forbid, if we had an emergency, no one was within driving distance. We had friends, sure, but there's a difference between being friends with someone and feeling okay about leaving your extremely young child in their care for a few days, or longer.

Still, I was grateful for my parents' help. Everyone had told me that my relationship with them would change after I had a baby—I just wasn't sure in what way. Some people found themselves disappointed by their parents' lack of involvement in their grandchildren's lives; others found their parents to be overbearing. But I had found myself growing closer to my parents after I had Henry. I had certainly developed more empathy for their experience as parents—they had had *three* children, and when she had me, my mom had been fifteen years younger than I was now. We don't become completely different people once we become parents, and I realized that I needed to understand them as people, too—not just as my parents.

I thought about this as the plane touched down in Orlando. I was relieved that they were able to watch Henry, which had allowed me to be able to join Kate at this conference. But I was also apprehensive about leaving him, in part because I was still nursing him three or four times a day, plus pumping. Still, my crazed nervous energy of the first few weeks of his life had given way to a somewhat less anxious state of being. Things had settled into a routine, more or less: sleeping, eating, playing, napping, pooping (*lots* of pooping). I was starting to get to know Henry's moods and what made him laugh. Right now, he was struggling to roll over from his back to his tummy, getting on his side like a little crescent roll and then getting stuck. He had a giraffe lovey that he was fascinated by. I still liked to put him in his baby carrier, snuggling him close and going for a walk.

As I checked into the hotel, I thought of something. "Do the rooms have freezers?" I asked the woman checking me in.

"No," she said. "There are refrigerators, but not freezers."

I frowned. "Is there anywhere I could store a small cooler?" I said, fishing it out of my bag. "It needs to stay frozen so I can store my breast milk." I was planning on pumping and then taking the milk back home.

"Oh!" she said brightly. "Sure. I can store it in a freezer in the kitchen, no problem." She took the cooler from me and I went up to my room. I was relieved that she hadn't given me a hard time about storing the cooler, but I was also slightly annoyed that the rooms didn't have freezers. Pumping—and transporting milk—had opened my eyes to a whole world of logistics that I had never had to remotely think about, starting with: Where do you pump? The co-working space where I did work sometimes had a room for pumping, which I appreciated, but I usually lugged my own pump from home because the one time I'd tried to use their pump, parts were missing. And not pumping when you need to pump is not optional. You can actually feel your boobs filling up and tingling, as though the milk is just preparing itself to squirt out of your nipple, and if you wait too long, the tingling turns into a rock-hard clog, and if you're *really* lucky, maybe you'll even start leaking through your clothes! But then once you're done pumping, you need to figure out where to store the milk so it doesn't go bad. The co-working space had a fridge, but if I was on the go, I usually brought a small cooler where I could store bags of milk. It was a whole other layer of things to think about.

And I often felt like my brain wasn't totally up for thinking about all the things I needed to think about. I was forgetful where before I had always been so on top of everything. I got easily overwhelmed; it was hard to focus. If I tried to work on something non-Henry related, his little face would materialize in front of me. Had I forgotten to feed him? Change him? Was he sad? Did he miss me?

The internet told me that this was evolutionary, that I was *supposed* to be consumed by Henry in the first weeks and months of his life in order to keep him alive. But it was hard not to feel like this was going to be my permanent state of being from now on.

When I got up to my hotel room, I had to laugh: It looked like it had last been renovated in approximately 1985, with vaguely colonial furniture and heavy drapes. My one night away from home wasn't exactly going to be a spa vacation, but I didn't care. I flopped down on the bed and turned on the TV. I didn't have to worry about getting woken up in the middle of the night by a screaming baby, or stumbling out of bed at six thirty to nurse. But I did have to pump. I'd finally invested in a hands-free pump—it consisted of two pods that went over your breasts, one on each side of your bra, and then suctioned the milk out; a slightly creepy but cool feature was that it communicated with an app on my phone via Bluetooth to tell me how much milk I'd pumped—so I popped it into my bra and turned it on. I sat back, propped up on pillows, and listened to the whoosh-whoosh of the pump as I flipped the channels.

THE NEXT DAY, Kate and I were on a panel about "the monetization of women's lifestyle content," where we talked about how advertisers were interested in paying to reach our audience. As the panel ended, I saw I had a text from my mom. "Where's Henry's formula?" she asked. We had a machine, kind of like a Keurig for baby formula, that we'd received as a gift from one of Matt's former *After Trek* co-workers. You pressed a button, and a bottle of formula appeared. It was magical.

Before I could respond, I saw she had texted me again. "Never mind—found it," she wrote.

"Which one did you use?" I wrote back.

"The one in the can next to the machine," she wrote.

I called her. "That's the wrong formula!" I said. "He uses the one in the box. The machine is calibrated for that specific formula, not the other formula."

"Well, it looked fine," she said.

"You have to take it out of the machine," I said, getting increasingly agitated. "He could get sick! I can't believe you didn't wait for me to respond!"

"I already gave him the bottle," she said. "He was hungry."

I was almost in tears. In that moment, I felt wholly inadequate as a mother: I'd left my tiny baby to fly across the country just to be on a panel? And now he was going to *starve* because I didn't produce enough breastmilk to have a stash of frozen milk, so I'd had to leave him with formula, and I hadn't told my mom *exactly* where to find the correct formula so she'd used the wrong one.

"Are you okay?" Kate asked as I met up with her outside the room where the panel had been held. I told her what had happened.

"Ugh, that's annoying," she said. "I mean, he's probably fine—is that okay for me to say?"

"I hope so," I said. "You know, 'they' "—I inserted air quotes—"make you so nervous about formula feeding in the first place, like you're somehow failing your baby. And, like, I've pumped and we've supplemented with formula from practically day one, so it's not like I have a *problem* with formula." I paused. "I guess I know, on a rational level, that he's almost definitely going to be fine, but I can't help but have these doubts. And I took it out on my mom."

"It's okay," Kate said. "Really. I would tell you if I thought you needed to worry, and I don't think you need to worry."

I nodded. I knew she was right. Everything about Henry took on outsized importance anyway, but even more so now that I was away from home. Then I felt the telltale tingling in my chest. It was time, once again, to pump.

A MONTH AFTER Orlando, at another podcast conference in L.A., I sat in the green room before my panel, desperately trying to clear my right breast of an extremely stubborn clog that just wouldn't go away. I was using a hand pump, pressing it into my breast with one hand and pumping with the other.

Then the door opened, and a confused-looking guy poked his head in and saw me partially disrobed on the couch. Apparently, the door did not lock. "Um, yeah, I'm just trying to pump in here, thanks!" I said. He scurried out. My boob was still clogged. "Fuck this," I muttered.

Before Henry was born, when I had envisioned what breastfeeding would be like, I'd pictured a bucolic image of Henry suckling greedily at my abundant breasts, the milk flowing easily into his mouth. Of course, we never had that breastfeeding relationship: The milk never flowed easily; most of the time he seemed like he'd rather be somewhere else. It was hard to stop, though—I kept going partly because I thought maybe *this* would be the time that we turned the pro-verbial breastfeeding corner. Maybe all the anguish and the pain and discomfort would one day magically disappear, and even if we didn't have the Instagram-perfect breastfeeding rela-tionship of my dreams, it would still be a calm, bonding mo-ment between us.

It never happened, and when he was around six months old, Henry started screaming every time I tried to nurse him, flinging himself dramatically off my lap to try to escape, and it was exhausting and demoralizing. I stopped breastfeeding and pumping a few weeks later. I had never felt so free.

CHAPTER THIRTY-EIGHT

"**M**y wife *loves* your podcast," the male voice on the other end of the call said. "I've listened to some of it, too, and it's great!"

Kate and I rolled our eyes at each other. We were on the phone with someone in business development at one of the major podcast networks that was trying to sign *Forever35*.

"We think you have a great opportunity to have ads on your show," he continued.

"Thanks," I said. "We do actually already have ads, so yes, I would agree. So what is it about our show that makes you interested in representing it?"

"Well, you're really hitting a demographic that is under-served in the podcast space," he said. I muted him and said, "Tell me something I don't know" to Kate. Back on the call, I said, "Right, but what about *our* show?"

He couldn't really answer the question. We'd been having these conversations for the last few weeks, and most of the time we were talking to men, like this one, who had never even bothered to listen to an episode of our show before they tried to hop into business with us.

I'd been selling ads on my own for the show for the last year or so. There was something exciting about it—it turned out, I loved making deals, and I loved telling advertisers what I thought we were worth, take it or leave it. They almost always took it. But we figured that someone who specialized in it could do even better. Hence these conversations.

But these phone calls were starting to get me down. They reminded me of everything in media that I had been trying to get away from—mediocre men who didn't prepare for the meeting, who expected to be able to coast on their entitlement, who thought that we should be grateful to just be in the room or on the call with them. For the past year, I'd been able to mostly avoid these guys, as Kate and I created the podcast we wanted to create, for the audience we wanted. If we wanted guests who came from a range of backgrounds, we could do that; if we wanted to take a stand and emphasize to our listeners that we were progressive, we were going to do that, even if we got angry emails from women who identified as conservative who thought we had abandoned them.

I felt lucky that I was able to have this kind of work environment, and I didn't take it for granted. That's probably one important difference between starting your own company in your twenties versus starting your own company at forty, or older: We don't have time for your bullshit, and we've seen a lot in the workplace that we don't want to replicate. We've been passed over for promotions, gaslighted and criticized, made to feel guilty for taking time off. But now we had the opportunity to create something different.

In the end, we signed with a company that had women in senior positions who loved *Forever35* and had actual thoughts about how to grow the show. We didn't sign with them *because* they were women, but it was eye-opening—to say the least—to see just how better prepared, on the whole, these women were, and how genuinely excited they were about bringing us on board.

As we were having these conversations, I thought about the life—the dream career—I'd left behind in journalism, the one that I had thought I was working toward my whole professional career. Now I would never be the editor in chief of a magazine or a website, but I'd found something better—something that, I was sure, made more of an impact on other people's lives, and on my own.

SOMETIMES I THINK about how I used to keep everything so private; like Harriet the Spy, my former idol, I was comfortable lobbing insults and criticisms at people in my own notebook, whether literal or figurative. But there came a point where I couldn't hide behind my notebook anymore. That's been a part of my growing-up process, I think. Being able to do what you love and get paid for it is a privilege, one that I like to think I've earned, and one that came about only through a lot of trial and error and getting to know myself.

So much of the day-to-day experience of being a woman is internalizing the idea that we need to camouflage ourselves, to adapt to the male-dominated culture around us; for women who aren't white, this is often literally impossible. I thought about all my male bosses, the meetings I went to where I was the only woman, all the times I felt like I needed to make myself smaller or less visible to gain the approval of men. I thought about all the mornings I got ready by blow-drying my hair and putting on a full face of makeup, and how I felt naked without it. I thought about all the carbs I didn't eat and all the hours wishing my stomach were flatter. I thought about all the conversations I replayed in my head, worried that I'd said the wrong thing. And I thought about how I wasn't that person anymore—she was still a part of me, but she was no longer my authentic self.

I have an appreciation for the person that I used to be, but an even deeper appreciation for the person I am now. I've learned that people will criticize you no matter what you do or what you say, and that sometimes their criticism is warranted, but a lot of times it isn't. As I've done this for longer—recording hours of podcasts where I'm basically just talking about myself each week, posting on social media, writing about myself— I'm getting better at determining when I need to course-correct or apologize, but also when I can tell myself that this person is projecting their own issues onto me, or that they're just flat-out wrong, or they're fundamentally uncomfortable with a woman talking frankly about uncomfortable subjects (and yes, often these people are women, too). It's also been a good lesson for me to learn that someone can criticize something I've done or said and the world doesn't end. And it's important for me, as I age, to stay visible and vocal, and to make other women's voices heard along the way, too—because not everyone is always able to speak freely (especially on social media) without criticism turning into threats of violence. Being able to show myself—my true self—to the world is a privilege, and one that I don't take for granted, and I believe that those of us who enjoy that privilege owe it to our fellow women to help them find their way there too.

Sometimes I can't totally believe it: I, who always felt slightly out of step with what I "should" be doing as a woman, helped create a community of people who not only accept me for who I am, but *look up to me* for who I am. Maybe all the stumbling through and making mistakes and feeling bad about myself for so long had been for a reason. Maybe being a late bloomer wasn't an accident. Maybe it was the *point*. I was a late bloomer *because* I had struggled to make sense of who I was and how I was meant to move through the world, but now that I'm here, and living out my late bloomerdom in all its glory, I can finally have empathy for the person I'd fought so hard not to be—and appreciate her, deeply. I used to worry so much about how I had "missed the memo" or wasn't doing things at the same time as everyone else, but now I see that it was only *because* I had had those experiences that I'm able to be happy and fulfilled.

It hasn't been lost on me that *Forever35* started as a podcast about caring for our skin—the most visible part of our bodies, and the body part that is judged and evaluated more than any other. I've come to see aging as a privilege, not something to run from or feel shame about, and coming to terms with this idea has given me a sense of self I never had. I now know that we don't disappear when we turn thirty-five or forty or fifty or sixty. We keep evolving and learning and growing, always right on time for whoever we are.

ACKNOWLEDGMENTS

I t's probably fitting that this book took a long time to figure out what it was, and even longer for me to actually finish it. I need to give a huge thanks to two people who helped me get it there: my agent, Alia Hanna Habib, who believed in it from the start, and my editor, Sara Weiss, whose incredibly thoughtful and perceptive edits made it a book. I'm so grateful to both of them for their support and, perhaps more important, patience. And a special thanks to Carrie Frye, who astutely pointed out that I was not, in fact, writing a book of essays—I was writing a memoir!—and guided me through some crucial rewrites.

I'm also very fortunate that the team at Ballantine is second to none: I get to have people like Carrie Neill, Debbie Aroff, Colleen Nuccio, Courtney Mocklow, and Jennifer Garza in my corner! I'm also grateful for the wonderful people at Gernert—Anna Worrall and Sophie Pugh-Sellers especially.

My life changed when we launched *Forever35*. Thank you, Kate Spencer, for being a better cohost and business partner than I ever could have dreamed of, and who put up with my endless schedule limitations and stress around finishing the book (during a pandemic!), and also for reading an early draft and giving me great notes. And thanks to all of the *Forever35* listeners who tune in week after week and trust us with their big life questions and their serum recommendations. We could not do the show without you.

Thanks also to Rachel Axler for giving me such astute notes on the manuscript, and to the members of W!W!W!, who had invaluable feedback on early essay drafts.

I'm so lucky to have such great, longstanding friends on both coasts. Thank you for your friendship and your love. (I hope you like the names I picked out for you here.) And thanks, also, to my new crew of mom friends, who have been such a crucial support system for me since Henry was born.

Our nanny, Holly, was a lifesaver while I was working on the book. Thank you for being there for him, and for me.

To my family: I miss you all so much, and I can't wait for us all to be together again soon. Thank you for providing me with material, and with love.

I'm so happy that Henry exists. I started this book when I was still pregnant with him, and I never could have guessed how much my life would change for the better once he was in it. Now I can't imagine my life without him. And, finally, my husband's faith that I would finish this book never wavered. He gave me pep talks when I needed them and reminded me that my life was, in fact, at least mildly interesting. Matt, you are an amazing partner and dad, and Henry and I are so, so lucky to have you.

ABOUT THE AUTHOR

DOREE SHAFRIR is the author of the novel *Startup* and the co-host of the podcasts *Forever35* and *Matt & Doree's Eggcellent Adventure*. She lives in Los Angeles with family.

ABOUT THE TYPE

This book was set in Garamond, a typeface originally designed by the Parisian type cutter Claude Garamond (c. 1500–61). This version of Garamond was modeled on a 1592 specimen sheet from the Egenolff-Berner foundry, which was produced from types assumed to have been brought to Frankfurt by the punch cutter Jacques Sabon (c. 1520–80).

Claude Garamond's distinguished romans and italics first appeared in *Opera Ciceronis* in 1543–44. The Garamond types are clear, open, and elegant.